ASPECTS OF
CHINESE
PAINTING

ASPECTS OF CHINESE PAINTING

by ALAN PRIEST

CURATOR OF FAR EASTERN ART, THE METROPOLITAN MUSEUM OF ART

THE MACMILLAN COMPANY

New York *1954*

ACKNOWLEDGMENTS

Essays I, III, IV, V, VII, IX, X, and XI are reprinted herewith by the kind permission of The Metropolitan Museum of Art; copyright, 1939, 1947, 1948, 1950, 1951, and 1952, by The Metropolitan Museum of Art.

The essay on the Tribute Horse is based on an article in the Bulletin of The Metropolitan Museum of Art and an article called "Journey to Pien Ching" which was published in *Asia and the Americas*, July, 1943. I wish to thank Asia Press for permission to use part of this article in its present form.

The quotation with which "Insects: The Philosopher and the Butterfly" opens is from *The Poems of Emily Dickinson* edited by Martha Dickinson Bianchi and Alfred Leete Hampson; reprinted by permission of Little, Brown and Company.

The opening lines of "Sung Landscapes: The Hanging Scrolls" are from "Nightingales" one of the *Shorter Poems* of Robert Bridges; reprinted by permission of The Clarendon Press, Oxford.

The opening lines of "The Horizontal Scrolls" are reprinted by permission of Dodd, Mead & Company from "Twilight," one of the *New Poems* by Richard LeGallienne.

We are also grateful to various museums and collectors for permission to reproduce their pictures, noted in each case in the illustrations.

FOR MISS AGNES PETERS

Contents

ASPECTS OF
CHINESE
PAINTING

1. Insects: The Philosopher and the Butterfly

"When landlords turn the drunken bee
  Out of the foxglove's door,
  When butterflies renounce their drams,
  I shall but drink the more!"
            —EMILY DICKINSON

ONE of the early Chinese philosophers, Chuang Tzu I think, once dreamed he was a butterfly and spent the rest of his life in worry lest he was in fact a butterfly dreaming he was a man. Both Chinese and Westerners smile at this seemingly innocent and beguiling fantasy. But if you stop to ponder on it, turning it this way and that, you will find it full of meaning, just as the ephemeral bubbles blown of soap and water, seeming no more than a brief diversion for the very young, in fact inform one of many things without the boredom of a wordy lecture. A gossamer bubble aglow with rainbow colors, floating on the lightest breeze and in an instant exploded— almost nothing, yet it is a completely perfect thing. Fragile and evanescent, it is a sphere like the sun and moon and the planet we live on and as such is a reminder of them.

Lightsome as it is, this philosopher-and-butterfly tale has in it one at least of the essential differences between the Chinese and the Western mind. The Chinese with tolerant amusement (and no science) accept a scheme in which, although man is superior, he is part and parcel of the natural world and of the universe. The scientific West does not yet do that. We in the West insist on making a sharp division between man and the animal world. We have long interpreted the first chapter of Genesis to mean that this world was created for man, that man alone has a soul. It is true that on our planet man both East and West has indeed achieved an ascendancy, but the East and West take very different attitudes about it. This feeling of superiority runs in the human blood; yet as far as one can see, the Chinese are less arrogant than Westerners—with the Chinese it is all part of one great harmonious

1

Flowers and Butterflies (detail), by Ma Ch'uan (*ca.* 1720–1800). Ex coll. Bahr, Metropolitan Museum of Art.

scheme. The Chinese man can be friends with a butterfly, not quite on equal terms but with a common understanding.

At just what point Western man began to take his lordly and patronizing attitude towards the animal world I do not know. Nor does it matter much. Somewhere along the line Western man has set himself up a little too high. How far does the Bible, Old Testament or New, really support him? After all, when there was trouble in the Garden of Eden it was Adam and Eve who were expelled, not the serpent. The Bible itself shows a great understanding of the natural world and is often friendly towards it. Surely it is man himself, Western man, who has grown toplofty in these matters. Medieval man was on friendly terms with the natural world. He saw clearly, and took great delight in, plants and animals and insects. He saw them as reflections, as mirrors of the Christian Church, but he was sensitive and sympathetic. Look at the illuminated manuscripts and read the *Four Mirrors* of Vincent of Beauvais.

"Hugh of St. Victor looking at a dove thinks of the Church. 'The dove has two wings even as the Christian has two ways of life, the active and the contemplative. The blue feathers of the wings are thoughts of heaven; the uncertain shades of the body, the changing colours that recall an unquiet sea, symbolise the ocean of human passions in which the Church is sailing. Why are the dove's eyes this beautiful golden colour? Because yellow, the colour of ripe fruit, is the colour too of experience and maturity, and the yellow eyes of the dove are the looks full of wisdom which the Church casts on the future. The dove, moreover, has red feet, for the Church moves through the world with her feet in the blood of the martyrs.' "

2

Flowers and Butterflies (detail), by Ma Ch'uan (*ca.* 1720–1800). Ex coll. Bahr, Metropolitan Museum of Art.

One suspects that the humanists of the Renaissance have a good deal to answer for in this and other matters. Certainly Western man's attitude has changed through the centuries. Observe the tremendous fuss Mr. Darwin created in the nineteenth century. That, of course, is very old hat now, but you will still find plenty of indignant people who do not want an ape for even a remote ancestor. I myself do not feel this way about it. My own great-aunt Martha, the terror of three counties, would have done far better as virgin queen of a tribe of chimpanzees than she did in ninety-six years of trying to straighten out Fitchburg, Massachusetts. Why must we in the West quarrel with the animal world? It is not at all necessary. We fight, we struggle, we make one exciting new discovery after another, such as that minerals are actually alive and changing, more slowly than plants or humans, to be sure, but still alive. The Chinese took this idea for granted long ago without scientific proof. How easy and how sensible!

If the philosopher-and-butterfly story can lead to such profundities, we may inquire further and consider the business of dreams. Webster's definition of a dream is "A series of thoughts, images, or emotions occurring during sleep; any seeming of reality or events occurring to one sleeping. Dreams are usually fragmentary and distorted representations of the experiences of waking life, though they are at times marked by consecutive reasoning or by a storylike naturalness."

> "We are such stuff
> As dreams are made on; and our little life
> Is rounded with a sleep."

Flowers and Butterflies (detail), by Ma Ch'uan (*ca.* 1720–1800). Ex coll. Bahr, Metropolitan Museum of Art.

"We are such stuff as dreams are made on"—Contemporary psychologists tell us that the human mind is in one respect like an iceberg. Only a fraction of it is visible to our conscious ego. The rest is submerged. Then which are we, the ninth above the surface or the turmoiling eight-ninths below? Surely we are both, and the dream is part of our mental fabric and life scheme. Chuang Tzu might well have been in doubt.

This business of dreams. Thousands of years of dreams. Take the dreams which disturb or enliven us in sleep. Until the twentieth century dreams were often considered as prophecies or illuminations. Then along comes Mr. Freud to tell us that dreams are our own wish fulfillment, and it seems that almost invariably dreams so interpreted are to one's discredit. Really, that man Freud has spoiled more agreeable dreams for us than anybody I know. And who until the detestable Mr. Freud came along did not in dreams enjoy running up and down stairs or floating happily or swimming in blue and golden seas? And suppose everything he says be true, for spoiling human pleasure nothing like it has been seen since the Spanish Inquisition. Begone, say I, let me run up and down stairs in my dreams. Let me dream I am a butterfly. What possible harm can that do anybody?

However, you need not dream of butterflies—you have only to look at a horizontal scroll of them in the Metropolitan Museum painted by a lady who signs herself proudly Chiang Hsiang Nu Shih Ma Ch'uan. In this she uses both her pen name and formal family name, the Chiang Hsiang Female Scholar—Ma Ch'uan—Ma being her family name and Ch'uan her first name. Ma Ch'uan was born in Ch'ang Shu in Kiangsu Province in the late seventeenth century and lived a good

4

Flowers and Butterflies (detail), by Ma Ch'uan (*ca.* 1720–1800). Ex coll. Bahr, Metropolitan Museum of Art.

eighty years. She is classed as a bird-and-flower painter—one of those convenient categories in use both East and West. China has had its feminists in plenty, and painters at least are not at all shy about it. Two of them painted the walls of one of the Buddhist cave temples of Tun Huang in the T'ang dynasty and painted kneeling portraits of themselves at the door of the inner chamber. The Chinese take none of the rather patronizing attitude of Western critics in regard to female painters but praise good painting irrespective of the sex of the painter.

Among her paintings this picture is a dream of butterflies come true—a ballet of butterflies, butterflies which appear by ones and twos and then in a whirl, butterflies in iridescent black, butterflies in pale creamy pinks and milky yellows and in whites painted upon white. No professional entomologist has been invited to name the species or even the general families because Western naturalists get very irritable when confronted with Chinese painting—Chinese painting looks realistic enough, but when it comes to animals and birds and flowers and insects it never quite conforms to Gray's *Botany* or Holland's *Butterfly Book*. This seems to put most naturalists into a fury. One botanist of my acquaintance took to drink and went quietly mad after a week or two of trying to determine the exact species of clematis intended by the Chinese painters. Not only he but one after another— whether they be zoologists, botanists, ornithologists, entomologists, or even geologists—are nearly all irritable in this matter. In painting we cannot catalogue Chinese flowers and insects with Linnaean precision, but even in the dullest Chinese painting of flower or insect there is a breath of movement, of the intangible thing called life.

Let us be content, when it comes to insects in Chinese painting, with their family names. Popular or scientific as you choose, the names of insects are usually attractive in any language. Take Female Scholar Ma Ch'uan's butterflies, for instance. Some of these airy creatures are related to the Papilionidae—the swallow-tails and their relatives, and to the Pierinae—the sulphurs and the whites, although, to be sure, many of these are in pastel pinks and dove blues (moonlight on snow the Chinese would call it)—the kind of liberty a Chinese will take with an insect, a bird, or a human being for that matter. Likewise, when we come to the Hymenoptera it is better not to struggle to pin a specific name to sawflies, ants, bees, and wasps. In the Ch'ien Hsuan picture at least two kinds of dragonfly appear—Odonata both. To the right one is tempted to recognize Anax Junius itself, and the dark-winged dragonfly is surely one of the Libellulidae. Pretty as are the Latin names of these creatures, for practical purposes the English common names will do—stag beetles, katydids, grasshoppers, crickets, walking sticks, and praying mantises, all conspicuous in Chinese paintings of the insect world. Usually they are associated with flowers and plants, as insects should be, but one subject often repeated is that of a seated cat, quiet and poised but with longing in its eye, as it watches a butterfly just out of reach—just barely out of reach.

In the West, indeed, insects appear in medieval manuscripts painted with sympathy and understanding, but where in Western painting is an insect painted for itself—as a kind of portrait as dignified as man is?

The Chinese make pets of insects, especially crickets, which they breed for singers or fighters. Do not think it is a matter of catching a cricket and expecting him to sing. The cricket fancier starts with cricket eggs. He hatches them on a corner of his own bed, which is made of brick and gently warmed. When the crickets are hatched they are carefully raised to maturity. As they mature the fancier listens and selects the most promising singers. He then consults a professional cricket connoisseur. The owner and expert give the crickets an attentive audition and groom a chosen few. A drop of hot wax placed dexterously underneath each wing is believed to smooth and heighten the quality of a cricket's chirp. No doubt it does so.

Furthermore, diva crickets live in gourds, gourds trained on the vine into various shapes, gourds with finely etched designs and pictures and openwork covers carved in ivory, jade, and fine wood, or worked in metal.

The diva crickets live in gourds, but for public performances they are transferred to small delicately constructed cages. Mr. George D. Pratt divided a collection of cricket cages between three museums, the Metropolitan Museum of Art and the American Museum of Natural History, both of New York, and the museum at Amherst College.

Flowers and Butterflies

(Detail). Ma Ch'uan, Ch'ing dynasty (1644–1912). Painting
on paper. Ex coll. Bahr, Metropolitan Museum of Art.

The singing of American crickets, whether those we hear in the meadow or those we hear in the house, is pleasing to some, displeasing to others. The house cricket is louder (and this is not a mere matter of acoustics), but few Americans would think to differentiate between individual singers in field or on hearth, much less make pets of them. The Chinese do.

Among Chinese crickets a favorite is the tiny insect called the Golden Bell. The Golden Bell is a country cricket and the subject of a legend. It sings in the country-side about the tombs of the Ming emperors and in the courtyards of the temples built in honor of the tombs. The legend is that one of the lesser consorts of the Ming court who could not hope to be buried with her lord found herself failing in health. One does not speak of death to an emperor. The consort sketched a tiny cricket—a portrait, she said, of herself. She died and was entombed alone. The emperor visited her tomb and was aware of a clear and delicate trill, as of a tiny golden bell. He searched and found a little cricket—the cricket of the sketch. This cricket is now known as the Golden Bell. In legend it is the consort who could not be buried with her emperor but preferred to become a cricket and sing in the fields about his tomb.

When I first slept on the temple terrace of the tomb of Yung Lo I did not know this legend of the Golden Bells but was aware of the rain of sound. Later, when I was living in Peking, Lao Sun in August would bring them in a shoe box, a thousand at a time, and turn them loose in the garden courtyards. Instantly there was a rain of sound, a fragile and delicate trill, gold but paper-thin gold. When hundreds of them sing it is a shower of sound—a shower shaken by the wind.

Alas, the Golden Bell do not live in Peking, free or confined. Water and tea were provided for them on leaves and in small saucers. Bits of lettuce and cucumber were everywhere, but each night the ghostly golden rain was less and less until in about a week they were gone.

Children, and grown-ups too, take too much for granted in this world. Until this minute it has never occurred to me to inquire how the Golden Bell crickets got to my courtyard at all. I cannot tell you whether Golden Bell crickets were commonly on sale in Peking's cricket market or whether Lao Sun sent a messenger to the tombs to catch them. The former is most likely the case, but on the other hand I never heard them in any other household in Peking, foreign or Chinese. (Poor Lao Sun, who has spent his years in devising entertainment for his friends, now caught by some Communistic vagary, philosophically says it is chilly in prison, he would like a coat.)

We have no painting of the Golden Bell cricket. But we have the Lady Scholar's picture of butterflies, and also the bees and wasps in the picture called The Queen Bee. This painting is attributed to one Chao Ch'ang of the Sung dynasty. This is

7

The Queen Bee (detail), attributed to Chao Ch'ang (*fl. ca.* 1000). Ex coll. Bahr, Metropolitan Museum of Art.

also a horizontal scroll. Whoever painted it had some fantasy in mind. He moves as a musical composer does, but he paints from right to left. His first theme would seem to be a very rambling pink rambler rose, his background for a swarm of bees. He goes on and repeats this rambler rose theme, the second time a yellow rambler rose and the second time pricked out with a community of wasps. It is subtle in its intent. We are meant to be dazzled by the flower painting and then realize that the flowers are merely a setting for the bees and wasps.

Both these pictures are near perfection as painting. One interested in authenticity can feel pretty safe that the butterflies are correctly dated and painted by the lady herself. The painter's name attached to The Queen Bee is little more than a name. Without a name it is still what is called a masterpiece. This I believe is a Sung picture, but I would not care if it were painted yesterday—yesterday or in the twelfth century, you cannot match it in known Chinese painting.

The Detroit Ch'ien Hsuan is another thing. I believe it is a Ch'ien Hsuan and the only one I feel sure of. All that is true and more. Not only is this Ch'ien Hsuan perfection as a painting, it is also a lovely glimpse of the insect world—as clear and seeming unconscious as an occasional line of Emily Dickinson. You must forget science—the juxtaposition of grasshopper, beetle, and katydid to the dragonfly family is possible but unlikely. This painter is chiefly concerned with the water world. Every child knows the water world, but as a man forgets that any pond, any pool, is a little world in itself, teeming with life, both visible and hidden. The painter reminds us. We can date the season exactly—late August—a partly eaten

8

The Queen Bee (detail), attributed to Chao Ch'ang (*fl. ca.* 1000). Ex coll. Bahr, Metropolitan Museum of Art.

lotus leaf and full-blown water-edge grasses would tell us this. In Peking the lotus comes into flower in early July; truck farmers harvest it in mid-August; in private pools, unharvested, it begins to wither and fade. And it is in the heat of August when the various dragonflies are at their prime.

Late August this picture, a poetic report of this water world, not of the great seas but of a pond—a pool. A lovely world—a world of dragonflies in flight, but lest we think it a dragonfly heaven Ch'ien Hsuan gives us a scrambling frog obviously bent on getting a dragonfly sandwich for tea.

For most people and for me, now, the content of a picture, a Chinese picture at least, often seems to give more pleasure than it is worth as a prized object of art. That is pure blasphemy and comes the more horrendous from a curator. I stand upon it. The presentment of a swirl of butterflies will attract the attention of the veriest lout as quickly as it will the erudite (and is more likely to be noticed by the former). To either it gives pleasure. The swirl of butterflies translated to a picture —are you yourself so full of vanity, so high-stomached that you think that this is a thing reserved to you? Somebody should tell you things and take you down a piece. Butterflies are pretty things, the sight of them gives pleasure to the stupidest prime minister and to the most brilliant clown. For each it is the same thing when you translate the butterfly to canvas or paper.

When the presentment becomes a work of art then all kinds of new things come into the discussion. There the anxious collector or curator must be concerned to acquire the butterfly painting that is the best, he must have it pedigreed and authentic. Collector or curator (the latter a public trust) does regard these things.

9

It is blasphemy to say they are of no account. They are of account, and collectors and curators perform, with all their errors and mistakes, a public service. Oh, yes. Oh, yes. A fine thing and to the public pride, but do not forget that in the humblest sketch that lovely creature the butterfly is there.

The attraction of butterflies for man is obvious, but insects which live in communities are also interesting to him, especially the bee and the ant. The bees, of course, established their communal life long before man arrived upon the scene at all and are likely to continue the same system for a long time to come. The bee does not change, but the attitude of human beings, particularly philosophers and sociologists, does. Victorian children were taught to admire the busy bee who, laying up a golden store of honey, acted as proxy bridegroom to the flowers, and constantly intoned a hymn of praise and thanks to its creator. In our century the bee and the ant were for a time pointed out as admirable examples of socialistic living. These days let any innocent senator praise the bee and he is immediately attacked as a dangerous Fascist. The bee naturally does not know this and persists in preserving its monarchial way of life with a dynasty that has lasted for countless millenniums and is not likely to be overthrown by any Marxian or Hitlerian bee.

Entomologists, of course, point out that on our planet it is a desperate race between man and insect as to which will ultimately inherit the earth. Already insects have developed a physical structure far more impervious to germs than that of man. They have learned to use as food every organic form of life and to protect themselves with germ-proof armor to an extraordinary degree. The entomologists do not joke. Farmers are more aware of this than city people.

You will have a glimmer of this yourself if you ever chance to meet a swarm of locusts—loathesome things. When first hatched they are tiny things. They grow rapidly and crawl day by day, fanning out across the countryside, devouring every blade of grass, every leaf. They grow, they crawl, they try their adolescent wings. They look like a seething flood of black lava, and from them rises a multitudinous, menacing sound. At last, their wings full-grown, they rise in a monstrous cloud and move to terrify new peoples and destroy new fields.

Man battling his insect enemies has discovered DDT—death to the insect world. This is a weapon to be used with caution lest in his triumphant war upon insect enemies he also kill off his insect friends and so deny the birds their food, flowers their marriage proxies, and eventually produce a desert waste which he himself cannot live upon.

The Chinese, unawakened to this danger, regard insects with tolerance and calm and did so long before Buddhism and the theory of the soul returning and returning in different form until it attained perfection became part of their thinking. With Buddhism came Ti Tsang, one of whose manifestations was as the Compassionate Lord of the Underworld. In Japan Ti Tsang became the gentle Jizo, who carries a staff with musically jingling rings to warn the insects of his coming lest he inadvertently step on one. A good Buddhist, bitten, will say nothing but smile upon the mosquito or the flea that bites him (even the pre-Buddhist paragon of filial piety, Wu Meng, slept naked by his parents' bed to distract mosquitoes from them). A Buddhist not quite so good, not quite so far upon the Way, may give the flea a cruel nip or slap the mosquito to extinction. But when he does so his conscience is like to trouble him; to take life is an error. To kill a mosquito suddenly and without thought is bad enough, but often your Buddhist deliberates; he may stop and consider the consequences—Shall I slap or Shall I not slap? This may mean another forty thousand years in hell, but this mosquito, she disturbs *me* now, and after all with the infinite years ahead forty thousand years do not matter much. Indeed, this mosquito on the same road that I am may very well be glad to get out of being a mosquito and perhaps reappear again as something pleasanter, a butterfly perhaps. Absurd? Not at all if you are a Buddhist or a Chinese.

A Western entomologist does not go so far as this, but he is on intimate terms with insects too and seeks to inform and interest the public in the insect world. He does so by articles in nature magazines, by occasional moving pictures, by photographic enlargements in which the house fly or the grasshopper magnified too many times becomes a monster so unbelievable that we give it a fascinated glance and go on to pictures of man-created mechanisms. Brilliant and colossal as are the various devices in a steel works, a paper works, a textile factory, man can look at them complacently—sensible and usual and indeed man-made—things of pride. Faced with a grasshopper as large as a steam roller we look upon it as an oddity, fascinating for a brief moment, something for a fancy dress ball or a festive holiday parade, or for the frightening fantasies of the Sunday comics. In vain do entomologists point out the extraordinary mechanical powers of insects, in vain point out the relative drawing power of the horse and the ant. Only the makers of airplanes seem to have a glimmer of the perfect mechanisms of the bird and insect world. They watch the movement of wings. They talk more of birds and properly envy them. They must watch insects also and either keep it a top secret or think it bad publicity. Their vanity is to be thought air- or birdmen. It is true that once in a while one may for a moment mistake a distant dot of plane for a gull or hawk. Only for an instant, until the eye informs one that the distant speck is not a live thing—beautiful but not alive. Much less do airplanes as they soar off the field at La Guardia resemble birds than they resemble insects, much more do airplane wings resemble the wings of insects than they do the wings of birds. More like dragonfly than hawk are those great planes as they roar across the sky above us.

Early Autumn (detail), by Ch'ien Hsuan (1235–1290). In the Detroit Institute of Arts.

Your passionate entomologist learns in dealing with his human associates to keep his love of insects a very secret thing. Even the Greeks, whose fantasies of faun and satyr, of centaur and minotaur, might well seem a little extravagant if not unnatural to modern man, paid very little attention to insects. There was, of course, the contest between Athena and Arachne over weaving. Arachne was punished and became a spider, and in the long run, wit you and tremble, Arachne has come off rather better. Who evokes Athena now? But the silken skein of one of the Arachnidae, crudely called the black widow spider, was much sought after in the Second World War for use in most delicate instruments.

In this I fall into the very error that I have pointed out that entomologists fall into. They know the wonders of the insect world—they try to entertain, to cajole their seeming stupid compatriots.

It is a difficult road. Your average human being considers insects as bugs, pests, except for butterflies and the larger night moths, which are pretty. He is right and can come up with a list of hateful insects, mosquitoes, gnats, spiders, house flies, roaches, death-dealing lice, and the unmentionable bed bug. Surely it is too much to ask him to consider such unpleasant creatures objectively, too much to ask him to observe the ballerina poise of the female mosquito that stings him. Too much to ask him to put sugar on the shelf for cockroaches as one puts out a salt lick for deer. Light and lovely on their legs, with delicate antennae like pheasant feathers on the headdresses of Chinese dancers, these roaches rush across your pantry shelf. So does your entomologist see them, and so you think him slightly or something more than slightly mad. He is not. He is fortunate—for there is hardly any place in the world, or any season or any time of day, where he may not find interest and entertainment. The rest of us would do well to emulate him as much as practical, to recognize the evil-looking robber fly and sinister ichneumons as

12

insect friends—friends because they destroy insects noxious and uncomfortable to us.

We will do well to consider spiders too, which of course are not properly insects at all but cousins to them in the sub-kingdom of the Arthropoda—Kingdom of the Jointed Feet. Spiders are our friends (even the few that are really poisonous will not bite unless disturbed). Their webs are wonderful and various, exciting to watch in the weaving, beautiful when complete.

No Chinese ever had such thoughts. Insects, as far as one can judge in painting or literature, they took quite calmly and at face value. They would seem, as far as pictures tell us, to have noticed them and painted them for pleasure. They did it well, so well that Westerners will look and accept with instant pleasure a praying mantis or a stag beetle in Chinese painting without thinking of them as nasty bugs at all.

2. Sung Landscapes: The Hanging Scrolls

"Alone, aloud in the raptured ear of men
We pour our dark nocturnal secret; and then,
As night is withdrawn
From these sweet-springing meads and bursting
boughs of May,
Dream, while the innumerable choir of day
Welcome the dawn."
—ROBERT BRIDGES, "Nightingales"

No one should, and few do, ask poets to be ornithologically accurate when they sing of birds; but it has always troubled me, for instance, to have that sharp-eyed observer Stella Benson pass off a flock of those small white-throated crows one sees in China as a flock of migrating starlings, and this in early September. For poets the nightingale is less an actual bird than the symbol of the poet's own heart throb; in poetry it is indeed a lovely bird. "Beautiful must be the mountains whence ye come," says Mr. Bridges, and then puts contradiction into the throats of the nightingales. "Nay, barren are those mountains and spent the streams," the nightingales reply. Once I lunched in a particularly small and unattractive oasis in Turkestan which was said to be famous for its tigers and its nightingales, but I neither saw the switch of a striped orange tail nor heard the feeblest chirp of any bird. Oh, poor sad nightingales! Where did they go? Back into the lovely lines of Keats and Shelley, perhaps.

One thing is certain: the nightingales did not go into the beautiful valleys of Sung landscape painting. In Sung painting birds appear almost portraitwise in pictures devoted solely to birds; they also appear as tiny grace notes in the long horizontal landscape scrolls—as items in the pageant of the day, the movement of the hours—where the painter, wishing us to enjoy the feeling of movement, includes birds in flight and human beings walking and invites us too to stroll in his panorama. But in the large hanging scrolls of the school called Southern Sung birds appear scarcely at all. There must be some reason for this and it may well be that, whereas in the horizontal scrolls the painter desired to convey the idea of hills and streams as they would be seen if the observer moved through them, in the large hanging scrolls he often wishes the observer to be in complete harmony with, and therefore completely quiet in, the particular scene to which he is invited.

The hanging landscape scrolls attributed to the Sung period, and more especially those of what is called the Southern Sung school, are supposed to be the expression of that contemplative phase of Buddhism called Zen in Japan and Ch'an in China. We have been told much of this philosophy and its symbolism. Often in these landscapes there is a scholar (or sometimes two scholars), very tiny in comparison to the scene he sits in. We are informed that we can gauge the profundity of the scholar's mind by the loftiness of the mountains in the distance. We are further told that when gnarled, ancient trees appear they are the symbols of the scholar's years; that, when hung with vines, the vines symbolize the chains of habit impeding the growth of the tree; and that when the painter calls our attention to a small picture of a morning glory, a flower which blooms briefly and fades, we are to understand that the morning glory which appears for an instant, the pine tree which appears for some hundreds of years, and the mountains which hold up their heads for almost countless millions are all one and the same—in the long run, each is relatively only a moment of time.

Such thoughts as these can make a human being feel very noble and wise if he accepts his place in this majestic scheme, or it can make him feel very ignominious and resentful if he does not accept it. And just there, in the attitude towards nature, is a great difference between China and the European West. The West—at least from the moment called the Renaissance (and perhaps from earlier times), when it decided man was not only the sole reason for the universe but also its ultimate purpose, and insisted on the importance of the individual man (and lately of the individual woman)—has taken the attitude that the forces of nature are on the whole inimical to man and are to be struggled against, titans to be chained. The West must attempt to conquer the winds with frail machines, harness the streams with brittle dams; it has even succeeded at long last in hatching that monster the exploding atom, which at the least scares almost everybody to death—all but the very brash who believe they can enslave it. Of this attitude you will find little or nothing in China. The West attempts to dominate nature. The Chinese accept it as they find it and seem to understand their place in the world as being part of it. They make no such sharp distinction between man and beast as the West does. The West does not allow that entity called a soul to any living thing save man. The Chinese believe that the soul, before it reaches perfection, may return and return

Landscape with Scholar and Attendant, style of Hsia Kuei (1180–1230), Sung School. Ex coll. Bahr, Metropolitan Museum of Art.

again; not only may your soul or mine return according to our deserts in the body of a better human being, it may return in the body of a venomous serpent or a monkey or even in a plant or a lump of jade. For the Chinese it is the same spirit force that lives in mineral and plant and animal. Hence the Chinese look upon natural things with an eye and feeling more intimate than is common to the West. The scholar seated under the ancient pine looking out upon the lofty hills is not alone; he is part of them and they of him.

These things are pleasant to know. It is also an interesting and productive entertainment to try to discover what the Chinese were thinking of and what they meant by the six canons of painting laid down by Hsieh Ho. It is pleasurable to contemplate the meaning of the "spirit resonance life movement," *ch'i-yun sheng-tung*; or of "naturalness," *tzu-jan*; "effortlessness," the *i*; "universal principles," the *li*; "bone means," *ku-fa*; "structural strength," *shih*; "pictorial reality," another character pronounced *shih*; "seasonal aspect," *ching*; "brush," *pi*; and "ink," *mo*. These searches and contemplations are the agreeable pursuits of Orientalists. Very fine pursuits they are too, but when almost all the scholars engaged upon them assure the reader that without all this and a good deal more there is nothing in Chinese painting for him and that he cannot understand a thing without it I am inclined to exclaim vulgarly, "Oh, go chase yourself!"

The essentials of this world we find ourselves in, and any pictorial manifestation made by any painter from the prehistoric cavemen down, are perfectly simple and available to anybody with eyes. One would have thought that all this patter about the mysterious East was outmoded long ago; but it seems to persist and break out with new virulence and new stupidities. In the lectures on art I have heard and in the books I have read I have never heard or seen it said that in order to admire the Sistine Chapel or the galaxy of saints in Orcagna's Paradise one must be either a Catholic or even a Christian; only scholars ask which saint is which or determine St. Catherine by her wheel or St. Agnes by her lamb. Then why, when we are confronted by the presentment of such simple things as hills and streams and trees with gentle scholars contemplating them, are we told that without a lifetime of study and research we cannot possibly understand them?

Is this not a silliness? Of course it is. Civilization and the human mind seem bent on weaving intricate webs and schemes and getting caught by them. One new, complicated fantasy after another they get up and call them sciences and humanities. While little men are bent on this the universe goes quietly upon its way. The sun rises and sets where it is bound to set, the moon waxes and wanes, and cleverer and cleverer as he grows man is unlikely to upset them much.

One room of the Metropolitan Museum is devoted to landscapes in the style of the T'ang and Sung dynasties. This is one of the most beautiful rooms in the world.

17

Here hang a score of great landscapes, mostly in what is called monochrome, painted on silk which was never white but which has darkened considerably with age; painted in ink, not ink as we know it, watery and pale, but ink ground down from hardened blocks of pure black, ink which when handled as the Chinese do is capable of variations and subtleties of shading far more telling, profounder somehow, than any play of color. The effect of a number of them is cumulative; they seem to catch light and spirit (*ch'i*, perhaps) one from another until in one comparatively small room a kind of magic is generated, and this small cubic square of space becomes so powerful that it stands out against, it displaces like a foreign body, the day and age wherein it finds itself assembled out of the past. It is an agreeable and curious experience to enter this room. More than in other rooms the noisy hum of Fifth Avenue is forgotten, and the outrageous roar of the airplane (a sound as evil as the whir of the dentist's drill increased a thousandfold) seems shut completely out. Just as the children in the Nesbit story could walk from their shabby London house through their amulet and find themselves in the past, so in this room one walks into China and the Chinese mind of eight hundred years and more ago. Here in the landscape paintings of the Sung school one will find the expression of the harmony between man and nature at its most harmonious moment. It is the school most admired by the Chinese themselves, a state of mind rarely if ever recaptured by them in later painting.

At the moment this school is out of fashion with the rising generation of Orientalists. It is always interesting to note changes of fashion. Just now the long-neglected Ming paintings have become the center of interest (and dazzling things they are too), but whoever would have thought that contemporary taste would turn and cast contumely on the monochrome landscapes of Sung, which even ten years ago were generally revered and sacrosanct? They still are, to the old and wise. But my astonied ears are assaulted with protests. I hear that in the first place almost no authentic paintings of the Sung dynasty exist and that probably none of these large hanging scrolls are either of the period or by the painters to whom they are attributed. This is bearable because nobody ever made great insistence on this point anyway. Granted that the names and dates of all of them are matters for dispute, whoever painted them or when, they are reflections dim or clear of a great school of landscape painting, and, as such, every one of them has value. But when I hear more, when I hear that Western connoisseurship was derived from the Japanese, and that the Japanese through all these centuries overrated Sung painting, and that Sung painting was at best, I gather, no very great shakes, then I am startled and cry "Halt!" A lion bitten by a mouse could be no more surprised than I at this idea. Goodness, one has seen Western taste in landscape swing from Corot to Courbet, from Courbet to Monet, from Monet to

18

Landscape, style of Hsia Kuei (1180–1230). In the Museum of Fine Arts, Boston.

19

Cézanne, from Cézanne to Van Gogh; but while taste changes, few contemporary critics are so rash as to tell us that Corot was no good at all—they will allow that Corot might come back to favor. Is Sung landscape painting about to be put on the shelf by a generation of vipers and our galleries filled with the stormy virtuosities or suave insipidities of the Ming and Ch'ing landscapes? I hope not.

The monochrome landscape paintings in the style called Sung were painted by men who liked being out of doors and liked to look at rivers and mountains. They set down with brush and variations of black ink the essence of the world they saw, and what they set down in a fashion simple and direct is available to any human eye. That phrase "the essence of the world they saw" is correct but a little too simple to explain what, although it is a very simple thing, seems to upset Western writers about Oriental pictures almost more than anything else. These writers, quite calm when confronted by the fantasy landscapes of Corot or Claude Lorrain, suddenly develop a postcard eye when confronted with a Chinese landscape. They find it profound and wonderful—the outcome of Ch'an contemplation and I do not know what all—that the Chinese painter, having learned to draw a mountain or a tree, does not confine himself to a postcard view but selects and sets down mountains and trees as he chooses; often when he gives his pictures place names—"The Eight Famous Views," for example—the scenes are recognizable, though they would not do for a geographical survey. And the scene is often beautiful. These are landscapes of the mind, poetical, majestic, free. There is no doubt that they differ from Western landscapes, but while this is partly an attitude of mind it is more a matter of practical things like selection and technique. Westerners, when they talk of painting, usually mean oil painting or at least fresco; it seems never to occur to them to compare line drawing or gouache to Chinese painting, which is essentially water color developed to an importance where it must be considered "painting." The Liber Studiorum of Turner and these Chinese monochromes I speak of have points of technique in common. Just as the Chinese learned to paint the suggestion of a particular species of tree, so Turner, more haphazard, learned to vary the forestration of a hillside so that one can pick out in his jottings different kinds of trees.

An essential thing in these Sung landscapes is, I think, that by choice the painters simplify and understate. Understanding clearly the nature of the various components of their landscapes, they choose the details freely and place them as they choose. They paint a shadowy outline of distant hills and put one pine or willow tree in the foreground and a tiny man. Each hill or tree or human being is by itself realistic enough (if by realistic we mean having an actual likeness), and the whole is in a sense realistic. We who look at these pictures may respond as one does to a line of poetry or a musical phrase.

20

Lovely as many of the surviving Sung paintings are, the young and avid scholar, aware that behind them must have been something more noble and more perfectly expressed, is apt to forget the qualities they have and, for want of a group of examples accepted as first-rate, condemn them all as secondary works of art. It is true that the most generous, the most optimistic, the most tolerant admirer of Chinese painting would be hard put to it to name ten large hanging scrolls of first quality which are generally acknowledged to be actually of the Sung period and even if of the Sung period to be of the best. In this matter opinions and taste differ. Some admire most the hanging landscape scroll in the Boston Museum once called Hsia Kuei and now primly called "style of Hsia Kuei," with any number of people ready to call it a Ming copy. This is a large, squarish picture, the subject of which is a massive hill, its lower levels hidden by mist, with a promontory, a group of wind-blown trees, a fisherman's net, and the fisherman himself following a path through the trees. This above all other of the larger landscapes is the best example of what East and West claim for the Sung school—a statement profound and simple of the majesty of the immortal hills and the relation of man to them. Thus the painter saw them, thus he set them down; this, he says in effect, is the way it is between man and wind and mountains, and that is one thing that the Sung landscapists gently repeat and repeat and repeat.

3. Sung Landscapes: The Horizontal Scrolls

"Yon mountain, vast as Behemoth,
Seems but a veil of silver breath,
And soundless as a flitting moth,
And gentle as the face of death,

"Stands this stern world of rock and tree,
Lost in some hushed sidereal dream,—
The only living thing a bird,
The only moving thing a stream."
—RICHARD LE GALLIENNE, "Twilight"

THE landscape paintings of Sung are not limited to the large hanging scrolls which, although they are suspect in matters of date and attribution, reflect the thought and principles of the Ch'an philosophers in so far as those philosophers chose to express in visual terms their calm and quiet contemplation of the hills and valleys about them. In the Ch'an world man is not only at peace with nature, he is part of it and knows his place. Mountains and streams, trees and winds and man himself are parts, and harmonious parts, of the same life stream. (Only recently has the scientific West discovered that minerals share with plants and animals the thing called life, this simple idea that the Chinese seem to take as a matter of course.)

While the same attitude of mind is expressed in the different sizes and shapes of Ch'an paintings—the hanging scrolls, the horizontal scrolls, and the album leaves —the visual impressions made by each form are so different that each, if we choose, may be considered separately.

Certainly the horizontal scrolls in Chinese painting are a special thing, with no good parallel in the West however we may catch at the faint likeness to panoramas and the like. These scrolls can run to any length, and it is notable that in the Ming and Ch'ing periods they grew longer and longer and were sometimes praised

22

Detail from a Yuan Dynasty version of a famous landscape by Hsia Kuei. A fourteenth century work attributed to Sheng Mou. Ex coll. Bahr, Metropolitan Museum of Art.

for sheer length much as the endurance of a taxi dancer or an aviator is praised and headlined in our day. There may be a use for endurance for twentieth century man. If he can stay in the air in a plane week after week over a given airfield it may be that later he can fly round and round the globe for sheer pleasure or to drop the latest bomb if his government thinks it a good idea; but the stars which stay in the firmament year after year with no apparent effort at all, and the arctic terns which twice a year wing back and forth between the poles as a matter of course, must smile if they think of it.

The length of a scroll may well impress us, but sheer length of itself should not be considered a virtue. What is more striking and more important is that in these scrolls the painters have managed to convey to those who look at them a sense of intimacy with the landscapes represented. Of course, the painters were intimate with these landscapes. Although the scenes often bear the names of actual places and often have recognizable features of the places whose names they bear, they are essentially the painters' own poetic fantasy of such places, part memory, part dream. And, just as dreams sometimes seem at the moment of waking more nearly perfect than reality, these paintings often have the quality of a dream brought clearly into the waking mind and set down on silk or paper.

One means by which the painters convey their intimacy with their subjects is to invite, to entice, the spectator into entering and becoming for a time part of the picture. The spectator must himself unroll and roll these horizontal scrolls, an action which immediately calls the muscles of his eyes into play. Hypnotists use this trick of calling eye muscles into play, but Chinese painters are more subtle, their purpose being not to knock the victim out but to lull him gently into projecting himself into the scene set for him. The trick works, too.

Detail from a Yuan Dynasty version of a famous landscape by Hsia Kuei. A fourteenth century work attributed to Sheng Mou. Ex coll. Bahr, Metropolitan Museum of Art.

More obvious but equally successful is the trick by which the painters influence us once they have lured us into their pictures. Again and again at the beginning of these scrolls a road or path appears, and we are almost bound to follow it. These roads direct the attention of the spectator and instruct his vision. Now and again he must walk in the foreground, viewing the plains and distant hills; then he is led on to the hills themselves, crosses bridges, climbs mountains, rests at high-placed temples; occasionally he may choose between the path and a boat, and often he is led completely out of sight behind a cliff or hill only to emerge farther along. This is a pretty trick indeed. So sure is he who follows the road that he is familiar with the landscape that he accepts the valleys and gorges which are not shown in the painting and is likely to offer to take camera shots on his next trip to any who doubt him. Just as you yourself, having descended a twisting mountain path and looked back from the plain from which only an occasional glimpse of the path may be seen, remember clearly pleasant vistas which you no longer see, so in these Chinese paintings you are equally sure of scenes which actually you never saw at all.

This horizontal form of painting, while immediately attractive to Western eyes, gives Western writers trouble. For one thing, our ordinary accounts of what a composition is or should be are difficult to apply to these scrolls which, if you choose to cut them into sections, are likely to present well-nigh perfect compositions wherever you cut them. The hanging scrolls and the album leaves can be subjected to Western rules of composition. The horizontal scrolls cannot. In them there is a concept of representation new to the West. The concept is simple enough really. It is representation which appears continuously, not in disconnected episodes. The painter of a horizontal scroll had in his mind a scheme for his painting

24

Detail from a Yuan Dynasty version of a famous landscape by Hsia Kuei. A fourteenth century work attributed to Sheng Mou. Ex coll. Bahr, Metropolitan Museum of Art.

of a river scene or a range of hills. Having his plan in mind, he started to work at the right end of his length of paper or silk. His first ten inches or so would already have been a complete picture if he had stopped, but he had no intention of stopping; he continued, and as he continued his mountain range or river gorge his picture grew as a vine grows, and finally the picture was done. After the event it may be seen that in his entire scroll there is a composition or a plan that we can measure by our accustomed terms.

Westerners are accustomed to having a picture confined neatly in rectangles or circles. We have as yet no terms for the composition that does not stay confined to circle or rectangle but moves from scene to scene much as a drop of blood pulses through its complexity of veins and arteries or as water follows its course from rill to brook, from brook to stream, from stream to river, from river to the sea. Here is something the Chinese have in their painting which Westerners do not have. The West has no handy word or phrase for this. "Movement" is part of it, but not enough. "Changing" is not enough.

The element in Chinese horizontal scrolls which does not appear in Western painting appears in Western music and Western poetry. But Westerners are so fond of pigeonholes that they firmly insist on different sets of principles for different arts; they view with distaste any analogy between painting and music, are somewhat shamefaced when they are forced to make such analogies. Painting is for the eyes—music is for the ears, we say; they must not be confused. A musical purist may frown upon a tone poem or an "image." A painter may not like to have musical terms applied to painting. But these Chinese horizontal scrolls invite musical terms, and both painters and musicians quite naturally use them. There must certainly be some common denominator in what we call the arts. We have

25

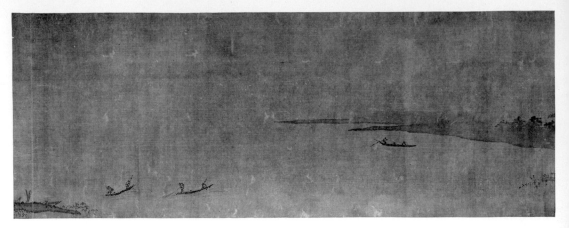

Detail from a Yuan Dynasty version of a famous landscape by Hsia Kuei. A fourteenth century work attributed to Sheng Mou. Ex coll. Bahr, Metropolitan Museum of Art.

five senses to inform us—the mind receives—but our minds insist on dealing with them as if they had no relation. They must. Most writing on aesthetics tries to prove they don't, or sets one art before another. But in this particular matter, the horizontal scrolls, the very terms that writers use quite clearly betray an intimacy between eye and ear.

In Philosophy 10 at Harvard, Dr. H. S. Langfeld explained to his classes the concept of empathy, *Einfühlung*, or "feeling into." Empathy means that when a spectator is introduced to a painting there is a brief moment, before he consciously begins to think, when unconsciously he almost identifies himself with the picture. The reaction differs from person to person of course. The concept is an easy one for the witty and frivolous to make game of. Just what, may say your wit, have I to do with a still life of a cabbage? If you inform him that, aside from his probable experience of seeing a cabbage and eating a cabbage, in a reposeful moment he has undoubtedly felt like a cabbage (a very agreeable feeling too), he may admit it but will yawn. If you put before him Duchamps's Nude Descending a Staircase he is likely to break into open rebellion. But the Nude Descending a Staircase has long ceased to be a clown show, and much has been written about the element it introduced into Western art. In this series of fractured rectangles the artist has tried to convey not only the movement of one human being descending a staircase but also a concept of the experience of descending stairs. He has done it and kept it strictly in his frame with a basic composition familiar to the Western eye. He has expressed it in violent and strident terms, and now the general public accepts and understands his principle.

It is just this element of continuous movement which, although new and startling in Occidental painting, Westerners have always accepted as a matter of course in

26

music and poetry. We accept the forms of music and poetry without question. We know perfectly well when we go to Carnegie Hall to hear Beethoven's *Eroica* that the performance is going to take approximately forty-five minutes. We do not expect to swallow Milton's *Paradise Lost* in one quick gulp. In such things we accept the fact that it takes time to listen or to read. But, having always expected to take in a picture at one quick glimpse, we squirm and wriggle at Chinese horizontal scrolls which in this respect make a similar demand upon us.

While we have no one word or phrase for this element, this common denominator of poetry and music and Chinese horizontal scroll painting, we can clearly see its essential character. We can understand it is a thing that moves as time moves (that is the heart of the matter), but it is time caught and captured as it moves through space, and measured in terms imposed upon it by the human mind—in sensory terms, visual, auditory. In music time moves measured and bespangled with starry sounds—bell and flute and violin. In the horizontal scrolls it moves defined in continuous visual sequence. In poetry it moves subject to both ear and eye: to ear when spoken, to eye when read. In all these there is also the indefinable element of the human mind stirring with immortal longings to be seen, to be heard, to be understood.

The idea of making a painting behave like a poem or a piece of music may be new and alien to us in the West and take a deal of explaining, but it seems to have been such a natural development in the East from very early times that the Chinese

Detail from a horizontal landscape scroll, Sung style, attributed to Wen T'ung (*ca.* 1050). Metropolitan Museum of Art.

27

Detail of landscape, attributed to Kuo Hsi (*ca.* 1020–1090). In the Toledo Museum of Art, Toledo, Ohio.

have never seen anything puzzling about it at all. After all, the Chinese wrote poetry on similar scrolls, why not paint pictures on them? And so they did from quite early times. We have accounts of landscape scrolls as early as the fourth century. There was as lately as 1927 in the Imperial Palace Collection in Peking a horizontal landscape scroll, labeled T'ang, which may appear again. From the Sung dynasty we have not only accounts of many painters who preferred monochrome but surviving paintings which bear their names and are certainly reflections of their work. It is clear that this category of painting was known in the T'ang dynasty (the Japanese include in their national treasure a hanging painting of a waterfall attributed to the great Wang Wei himself) and developed with prodigious variety in the Sung dynasty.

The distinctions and divisions made by Chinese writers centuries after the period of these painters have interest, but surely all this monochrome landscape painting can be considered part of one movement. Technically the Chinese call Ma Yuan, Hsia Kuei, and Kuo Hsi court painters, but for Western purposes Fenellosa was essentially right to include them with the Southern Sung painters. Better perhaps to call the pictures in this category Sung monochrome landscape painting. In any case, it is all part of the same thing—a school of landscape painting so beautiful and powerful that after a thousand years its influence is still strong in both Chinese and Japanese painting.

As for the horizontal scrolls, so dour and grim are contemporary scholars that they will not allow a single one of them to be original, and most of them will not allow them to be even of the period. Though experts may quarrel as to exact date and attribution, from the scrolls that survive, even if we cannot prove they are by Hsia Kuei or Ma Yuan, we can get a very clear idea not only of particular subjects

28

but of the school as a whole. Consider and view when you can such scrolls as the Boston Tung Yuan, the Kansas City Hsia Kuei and Hsu Tao-ning, Freer's Kuo Hsi and Ma Yuan, Toledo's Kuo Hsi snowscape, the Chinese Government's Hsia Kuei, and the Metropolitan's Wen T'ung, Kuo Hsi, and Yuan dynasty version of a Hsia Kuei landscape. If you will look at these you will get a very good idea of Sung landscape scroll painting of the Ch'an school.

Don't quarrel. Enjoy what we have. Once I traveled with a formidable lady. She found the Japan Inland Sea a little like Bar Harbor, but it did not smell so pleasantly; she surveyed the lion-colored shores of Shantung and compared them to their detriment to the Greek Islands; when beside the train the crenelated walls of Peking burst upon us she remembered the walls of Constantinople. No Ch'an philosopher she. Hawthorne was always finding fault with places; Ruskin was inclined to carp. Why must your traveler confronted with Pike's Peak immediately disparage it for not being Mount Everest? Why look for trouble? Why find fault with these beautiful Chinese scrolls?

Do not ask for a master painting. Those attributed to Ma Yuan, to be sure, have peaks that tower like stalagmites; those attributed to Hsia Kuei have mountains domed; those attributed to Fan K'uan have receding rocky masses. But all these particular things may appear in one painting to which is attached any handy name.

The play of rushing stream and mountain gorge that is most often repeated refers again and again to the Thousand Miles of the Yangtse by Hsia Kuei. The most famous version of this picture is the Imperial version which is catalogued in the Chinese Government Collection. Some claim this to be original. The really cynical, pointing out the possibility of substitution, insist that it is as late as the eighteenth century. Do not argue the point. Take this and the other scrolls we know and enjoy the composition; observe the title; observe the mild complacency of a painter who states he will set down a thousand miles in a very few feet— not only says but does.

4. Sung Landscapes: The Album Leaves

"Adieu! the fancy cannot cheat so well
As she is fam'd to do, deceiving elf.
Adieu! adieu! thy plaintive anthem fades
Past the near meadows, over the still stream,
Up the hill-side; and now 'tis buried deep
In the next valley-glades:
Was it a vision, or a waking dream?
Fled is that music:—Do I wake or sleep?"
—JOHN KEATS, "Ode to a Nightingale"

THE same approach to the natural world is evident in the three physical forms of landscape painting of the Sung school, the hanging scrolls, the horizontal scrolls, and the album leaves; but the very difference in size and shape invites a different response upon the part of the spectator and actually stimulates different muscles of the eye and mind. One must view from some little distance, standing or sitting, the large vertical scrolls and look at them almost as if one were in the same landscape, only a little farther removed than the figures represented in them. The proper way to look at the horizontal scrolls is to sit at a desk or table and take part in the picture as one unrolls it from right to left, rolling forward or back at will, looking at just the expanse of the changing scene that one finds most pleasing. Unfortunately this practice is not possible in a museum gallery, and the spectator must work a little harder by moving himself instead of moving the picture and by bending his eye to the angle it would have if he were sitting at a table. For these pictures were painted. The painters who made these pictures worked with their eyes at just that distance from silk or paper, and if we are to see what a given painter saw we must adjust our vision to his. The third form of Sung landscape painting, the album leaves, which include flat, round fan shapes some of which were actually used as fans and later mounted as album leaves, to be seen at their

Sailboat in the Rain, album leaf by Hsia Kuei (active *ca.* 1180–1230). In the Museum of Fine Arts, Boston.

best, and as the painter intended, should be looked at as if one were sitting at a table and turning the pages of a book, or as if one were holding a book conveniently in one's lap and bending over it. All this is so obvious that to set it down in cold black and white instantly appears to be almost puerilely didactic. But the great majority of Westerners see Chinese paintings only in the galleries of museums. They have not had the agreeable experience of handling a horizontal scroll themselves or of turning the pages of a Chinese album. They see these things laid out in a case or hung upon a wall, the horizontal scrolls extended, pinned down, bereft of movement, the album leaves stuck up like postage stamps. It is the difference between seeing a live panther and seeing a panther skin nailed to a barn door.

Having written this little preachment down, I view my own words with the same exasperation that I feel on reading Stella Benson's request to the reader of her *Far-Away Bride* that he read the book of Tobit in her appendix before beginning the story. If I dance with rage to be told by Miss Benson to read Tobit I should be prepared to have my ears boxed when I have the impertinence to tell the reader of this book how to look at Chinese pictures. To tell the truth, I never stopped to think the matter out before in just this way, and I am so pleased with what is a discovery for me that I should like to hand it on.

Pictures hanging on a wall, pictures to be unrolled upon a desk, albums with leaves to turn, three pleasant things; which pleases most is according to each one who looks, according to time and place and mood. Of the three, the album leaves are the most intimate, and as we look and wonder and imagine what this Sung school really was at its best, as we worry about dates and attributions, the heart of the secret and the answers are waiting in the album leaves.

There are myriads of album leaves in the Sung style; among them must be many that were painted during the Sung dynasty, some with correct signatures. Sooner or later we shall surely arrive at an agreement on some as actually Sung and on just who painted which. The matter of physical survival enters into this. The large hanging scrolls were apt to be hung for periods of considerable length. They were used more often. Their very size made their preservation more difficult. The horizontal scrolls were taken out and unrolled occasionally. Every unrolling takes its toll, and wise owners were careful of the best ones and unrolled them rarely. Some of the hanging scrolls and some of the horizontal scrolls might be stored away and, half forgotten, have long periods of rest. Both are very vulnerable. But the album leaves, small rounds and squares, never hung or long exposed, protected by blank pages and heavy covers of wood or layers of paper mounted with brocade, could be looked at year in and year out with a minim of wear and tear.

It is true that the album leaves were easier to copy than the scrolls. Through the centuries almost any painter might try his hand at painting a Hsia Kuei or Ma Yuan (adding the signature for full measure), some of them succeeding so well that even in our day an album leaf by Prince P'u Ju with the help of a little staining and sun rot might easily be collected by the unwary as a Ma Yuan. True enough, but equally true that among the myriads of extant album leaves many are actually Sung. View the activities of Ch'i Pai-shih, one of the greatest of contemporary painters. His shrimps please everybody so much that at the age of ninety not only does he repeat himself half a dozen times a day, but his contemporaries imitate,

Bare Willows and Distant Mountains, album leaf by Ma Yuan (active *ca.* 1190–1225), Sung monochrome school. In the Museum of Fine Arts, Boston.

copy, and forge his paintings and even his signature until his shrimps seem to
breed faster than real shrimps in the sea. If you stop to think of the probable
shrimp census or even of those shrimps which have been personally presented to
you and devoured, you will probably be quite frightened by the number; indeed,
if you think of the number of shrimps too much you are likely to end up in a padded
cell. Don't think of them too much; think of them just enough to see that if Ch'i
Pai-shih can paint shrimps from morn till night it is quite possible that a Sung

painter, having achieved an album leaf that pleased him, painted it more than once —perhaps a score of times—so that if we find twenty similar leaves all of the same subject, all attributed to the same master, all with the same signature, it is not to be insisted upon that one is the original, the other nineteen forgeries. It is quite possible that the same painter did all twenty of them himself.

It is in the album leaves—these agreeable rounds and squares, most commonly about ten inches across—that we arrive at the heart of Sung monochrome landscape painting and see and feel as clearly as if we ourselves lived in the twelfth century; the silk may have darkened a little with age but not enough to obscure our sight. When we look at the finest of these we are looking without a shadow of a doubt at Sung painting at its best.

The size of the album leaves is small, but they are not in any wise miniatures. One after another has the quiet splendor of scale which we find in the hanging scrolls. These album leaves are not little things. The best of them are very great paintings, set down in terms comfortable for the human eye. (Reinach's *Apollo* gives intimation in postage-stamp size of the grandeur of Titian's Assumption or Tintoretto's Milky Way.) The human eye is nimble as a monkey. The human eye looks as it pleases, it lives a life of its own; and so valuable is it to us who sit in darkness, more helpless than a jellyfish without our senses to report and inform us, that we give it a good deal of latitude. Our eyes are our most exciting messengers. They are the most agile reporters in the history of mankind. In the present case the eye will report that the Sung album leaves are little only in the matter of inches. They are not small things; they are large things. The painters of the album leaves, perhaps unconsciously and perhaps without plan, hit upon a means of expression which holds good century after century. Photography is rather recent (the camera was not a nuisance in the Sung dynasty). Contemporary man with monkey eye looks at a small photograph of the Jungfrau and juggles it without much trouble into scale. But the Sung painters produced a form of painting which would reduce a mighty mountain into terms the eye could understand then and can understand now.

There never has been a more beautiful or noble school of landscape painting than that of the Sung monochromes. Just at that time, just at that moment, painters for a little space saw, not only saw but understood, not only understood but were able to set down by the simple means of ink on silk or paper for the eye to see, and for the eye to inform the mind, simple and profound truths. Just at that moment these men clearly saw the law and the pattern of the world in all its inexorable majesty. They saw more: they saw and understood man in his relation to it. They saw it then, and their record is not lost. Even if there were no painting left which we could call surely Sung, even if we had only dim reflections, we too could see

Snowy Landscape, album leaf of Sung monochrome school. Ex coll. Bahr, Metropolitan Museum of Art.

and understand. The Greek archaeologists have to guess at lost Greek paintings from echoes on vases, in literature, and in garbled later paintings. A Greek archaeologist might well stare enviously at the complaints of a Chinese archaeologist—we Chinese really might complain that we have too much.

In the album leaves the promises which are in the reflections of the hanging paintings and the horizontal scrolls are fulfilled. From them you may make your judgments and demands upon the larger paintings. There are album leaves in Boston which are called "by Ma Yuan" and "by Hsia Kuei," not "attributed to," nor "after." Take them as standards, and if the larger paintings or other album leaves do not approach them in quality then you may suspect them. Let us not enter into controversy or names at all; it is not necessary for pleasure or understanding. But let us repeat and repeat again that here in the album leaves is the pure jewel that all our writers East and West are searching for. It is here, not in isolated fragments but in small, perfect things repeated again and again, as clear and lucid as the drops of dew that will appear on the lotus leaves of this year and be collected just as they were in 1150 by the tea drinkers of China. The thing we have sought for is here. It is as simple as so many things—as Newton's apple, for instance. Once it is put in words everybody says "Of course; it is so obvious why bother to say it?" This is one of those things.

Pay no heed to the yap and snarl of scholars as to who painted what and when, nor to their gloomy howls against the moon that Sung painting is lost. It is *not* lost; it is present in the scrolls and in almost innumerable album leaves. This country is lucky; in the Boston Museum of Fine Arts and in the Metropolitan—take the two—one example after another of the "lost" school of Sung exists in such variety that we are able to see in brief dimension much if not all of its subject matter and the peak of its performance. Here we can see, caught in a small space, mountains rounded, mountains sharp, mountains in sunlight, mountains in mist, mountains in summer, in winter, spring, and fall. We can see the perfection of a particular tree, the rush of water in a stream, and, swirling in vapor, that strange and wonderful creature the Chinese dragon, which is the seed and the soul of mist and rain, of moving water, and also of the mind powerful and free. *Lung t'iao T'ien Men*, "The dragon leaps past Heaven's gate." The symbolism is explicit; the great carp, like a salmon vaulting the rapids, already shows dragon whiskers and passing the gate of Heaven becomes dragon at last, no longer bound to struggle against the rushing flood but free to move wherever water is in any form.

And in the album leaves the birds appear, numbers of them. We must not forget that while we speak of the major theme of the Sung monochrome school, landscape and man's relation to it, the Sung painters stopped to look at particular birds and flowers and painted them with the dignity usually given to portraits. When we attend the landscapes we scarcely find birds at all in the large hanging pictures and find them only as grace notes or indications of movement in the horizontal scrolls, but we occasionally find them in the album leaves. Suddenly in an album leaf where the bare, ruined choir of branches would seem to be enough we find a pair of magpies or a flock of white-collared crows, noisy things in real life; but here, although silent of throat, the variety of movement, the flash of wings affect the eye as the agreeable cacophony of an orchestra tuning up affects the ear. In such album

36

Magpies on a Wintry Bough, album leaf attributed to Ma Yuan (active *ca.* 1190–1225), Sung mono-chrome school. Ex coll. Bahr, Metropolitan Museum of Art.

leaves the birds appear as part of the landscape just as in other album leaves men appear each in his relation to the whole scheme of nature.

Look to the album leaves, my younger friends, and do not let your eyes become beclouded nor your minds befogged by the contentious, pessimistic prattle of professors. Look at the album leaves. There is the "lost" Sung painting, pure and serene as light at morning. There it is. Add to the album leaves the information in the horizontal and vertical scrolls and you will have your Sung dynasty ink landscape painting, as familiar to you as Central Park. Lovely, lovely, lovely are

37

these pictures. They do not need explanation or meaning. They may be accepted lightly as one accepts and takes pleasure in the light of afternoon.

Light—air. Air, that seeming weightless nothingness so weighty that it supports the suns and moons and the stars of the universe and keeps them in balance. Air, that seeming lifeless nothingness so charged with life that it can explode into a burning spark, a spark which may become a flaming entity. Out of the seeming empty air a spark, out of the spark an amorphous ball of fire, and the never-ending cycle has begun. Out of the flame a sphere of molten mineral and steam. The mineral cools to rock, the steam to water. The ceaseless play of water on the rock brings earth; lichens appear and, with increasing speed, plants, reptiles, birds, animals, and at long last man. And all of these, from the long-lived rock to short-lived man, at last return to the air from which they come. This is the never-ending cycle on our particular planet. It is governed by inexorable laws which we prying humans learn more and more about. Majestic and awful is this scheme, pitiless and proud.

Very lofty and beautiful, but not, alas, satisfactory (and what philosophy is?) for the teeming billions of human beings who struggle for existence and do not like to be told that they play any such humble role in the universe. They do not like it a bit. My great Aunt Charlotte would have made short work of the Ch'an philosophers, and I myself find it difficult to maintain such composure as theirs on those days when I have an aching tooth or am harassed by my landlord, who quite evidently cares not a whit about Ch'an philosophy or whether I am hot or cold. Indeed, once I did see one of the great Ch'an abbots, usually tranquil and serene, lose his temper and beat a countrywoman about the head with a broom. He jumped up and down like a gorilla, red robes flying. This I saw by peeking through the windows of the peaceful chambers of my guest apartment with startlement and horror. An hour later the abbot was as serene as ever, turning the pages of holy books. I dared not ask how such serenity could be upset, but I took pains to find out what upset it. There were bandits about. The countrywoman had accused him of telling the bandits where her donkeys were hidden, to keep them away from the monastery's donkeys. From this I deduce that noble as philosophy can be, far as your philosopher can see, aeons ahead, aeons behind, he is likely to be caught and irritated beyond endurance by the tiny frets of contemporary life.

There are contradictions always, but there is no doubt that through our human history men alone and men in concert have immortal longings and now and then achieve nobility and leave a record of it. Here in Sung painting is one of those achievements. The Sung painters, especially those under the spell of Ch'an Buddhism, achieved one of the noblest and purest expressions of a tranquil understanding of the physical world we live in and, by implication, of the universe.

38

The whole thing sums up very simply. If one (not me) is so presumptuous as to write a history of art one sees that now and again there appear enduring manifestations of one art or another. We of today are aware of the splendor of Egypt and the glory of Greece. We are aware of the grandeur of Rome and the ecstasy of Chartres. Sung painting—especially the monochrome landscape paintings, catalogue them as you will—is one of the most noble records in the history of man.

5. Landscapes: Green and Blue

LANDSCAPES blue and green—or green and blue—are landscapes in which blue and green predominate. It is an arbitrary classification, invented by the Chinese, useful for descriptive purposes. The long tradition of monochrome painting can also be isolated as a phase of Chinese painting by one characteristic, that it is a tradition in one color—if one is willing to consider black and its myriad variations as a color. But Chinese painting is not confined to monochrome. It ranges from painting done in ink to painting mostly in ink with touches of color, to painting in a full blaze of color. And it did not begin with one and progress to the others; all three were clearly apparent in the T'ang dynasty and have run parallel courses ever since.

Landscapes in green and blue were a recognized form of painting as early as the seventh century. The first great painter of these was Li Ssu-hsun, born in 651, a grandson of a nephew of the first emperor of the T'ang dynasty. He was "the first great painter," but his technique was derived from the sixth-century painter Chan Tzu-ch'ien. It is possible that Li Ssu-hsun added to the blue and green the gold outlines which sharpen the mountain and rock forms and make them glitter. In any case we put him at the head of a tradition which survives to this day.

"He painted the surface of things and did not probe the meaning that lies hid within." For the moment let us not quarrel with that remark. The great monochrome landscape painters certainly probed the meaning that lies hid within. It is true of all of us, East and West, that we are more aware of the outlines, the bones, of the mountains on a gray day than when they are in full spring colors irradiated by sunlight. It is possible that the painter dazzled with color is diverted from the meaning that lies within to the richness of the surface. Possible, and for the moment let us agree with the Chinese writer—agree but not condemn the "surface of things." If the paintings of Li Ssu-hsun reflected the gaiety and glitter of the palaces and court and placed them in landscapes gay and glittering let us accept that as the lively thing it is and not moralize about it.

The painters of green and blue have left us very pretty pictures. The paintings ascribed to a particular painter give us an understanding of him and his presentation of the world. There is no authenticated Li Ssu-hsun—but the British Museum painting, the Goloubew painting in the Boston Museum, and an album leaf in the Metropolitan Museum inform us of a world of fragile palaces with richly clad but tiny human beings set against a background of mountains green and blue, often etched with gold. A miniature style, if you like, but a miniature can be fine painting. Do we not catalogue the Duke of Berry's Très Riches Heures as miniatures?

Are there not many aspects of this world we live in? While we for convenience catalogue and judge, while we treasure the pictures of the past can we not see in our Western art that the Très Riches Heures and the Sistine ceiling are both the work of genius, both the work of painters who saw with both mind and eye and were able to set down what they saw better than most of us can?

The Chinese paintings of the green and the blue have had a long history since Chan Tzu-ch'ien and Li Ssu-hsun. Through the centuries these names and others have become tradition. Li Ssu-hsun of the seventh century is considered the founder. We hear of Li Chao-tao, the son of Li Ssu-hsun, and of the Sung painters Chao Po-chu and Chao Pao-hsu. In the Ming dynasty we have Ch'iu Ying, who was so famous that for centuries his name has appeared on uncountable paintings of charming scenes. Not yet famous in the West, we have in the eighteenth century Kuan Huai, who painted at the court of Ch'ien Lung, painted as skillfully as his seventh-century predecessor and perhaps with a greater understanding of the "meaning that lies hid within."

We have a history of the painters of blue and green. Where may we see examples or reflections of them? For Li Ssu-hsun himself look at the British Museum painting of the Ch'ang Lo Palace illustrated as frontispiece in Arthur Waley's *Introduction to the Study of Chinese Painting*. Look next at the Goloubew picture of the Ch'iu Ch'eng Palace, in Boston, once attributed to Li Chao-tao and now to the late Sung dynasty, and third at the large album leaf of palaces in the Metropolitan. None of these are considered originals but all of them are clues to the originals.

When it comes to the Sung dynasty, greater claims are made for Chao Po-chu. There is a long processional in Boston, there are three paintings in the Metropolitan, a faded scroll of palaces, a dazzlement of green peaks, and the ravishing miniature of the Bahr collection. Do not stick upon a name. Authentic or not, from these we get glimpses of the painter and his period. They are all valuable.

Contemporary connoisseurship is bent on facts. Which of the Giotteschi painted which picture for a certain church on a certain date. Nice comfortable system, something reliable, something understandable, something one can get one's teeth into. Dates and places are important to us—a way of orientation. They are safe, something we all agree upon, comfortable. But is the matter of dates and facts all-important for the human being passing through for a little time as centuries come and go? Is it not possible that you or I, without dates and cataloguing, can take the same pleasure in a green and blue landscape now as a Chinese did in the seventh or eighth century? May we not take pleasure in the "surface of things" as well as an eighth century Chinese?

The study of color is a heady business. By this I do not mean the explanation of color by means of long and short wave lengths, nor the logical cataloguing of primary colors in the order and interrelation with which they burst forth from the facets of a diamond or appear with the illusion of solidity in a rainbow, nor yet the charts and solids (as of Denman Ross and A. H. Munsell) with which we instruct the young, but rather the effect of color upon the individual human eye and upon the mind behind it. It is said that the human eye can differentiate between nearly a million different hues and intensities, a truly breath-taking number when one considers that we start with six colors, yellow, orange, red, violet, blue, green. If we add the six intermediaries (orange-yellow, red-orange, and so on), making twelve, and carry them each through nine degrees from white to black (white and black counting as two) it adds up to only eighty-six. Even when we take the eighty-four that lie in these sequences from white to black and carry them through four degrees of fading to an indistinguishable neutral, we arrive at no more than three hundred and thirty-eight. Your student who has himself done the labor of producing three hundred and thirty-eight variations of color quite rightly feels he has achieved something and certainly is aware of more colors than he was at the start. Soon he learns that while this has the safe look of a multiplication table it does not act like one. In theory he should be able to write a foolproof description, RO, HL ¾ N (red-orange high-light three-fourths neutralized), let us say, and send it to a painter in Patagonia or Timbuktu in the comfortable belief that his friend there can reproduce the exact color. It does not work. The trellis upon which he hangs his scales glows and shimmers with the nine hundred thousand possibilities that lie between the points he has charted. The guide is trustworthy as far as it goes, but it bears the relation to the whole that a time-table map bears to a geodetic survey. At that it is safer than visual memory, as anyone who has tried to match silk or wool without a sample knows.

Spring Morning at the Palaces of Han

(Detail). Attributed to Chao Po-chu, Sung dynasty (960–1280), twelfth century. Horizontal scroll. Painting on silk. Ex coll. Bahr, Metropolitan Museum of Art.

When we turn from the comparative safety of color definition to the emotional effect of color on the individual, we are on no man's land, and there it is each man for himself. Yet there are conventions, associations, fashions—for instance, a widespread belief that the brighter reds are exciting whereas the deeper blues are soothing. There also seems to be an idea in our country today that gray and white and faded mustard are the hues best suited for our apartments and houses. Primary colors, say we, are the choice of primitive, barbaric peoples, entirely forgetting the Eskimos, the pallor of whose igloos we seem to imitate. And by common consent a society will give a color a meaning—the Chinese mourn in white, we mourn in black—the Chinese make red a happy color used for wedding dress, we associate it both with courage and with sin. Do these selections express a psychological reaction to color itself or are they chance and arbitrary conventions set down by lawmakers as were the rulings for the colors of court robes in China?

The multicolored vegetable and animal kingdom, except for the human species, pays very little attention to color at all. It would seem, then, that if color is a mystery it is another one of those man-created puzzles, and one would be inclined to think that if red has become the color of Satan and the inferno and black the color of sadness, it is man who has attached these meanings to colors, which are entirely innocent by themselves. Then the emotional effect on human beings would be the result of their mental associations with a color.

As to the individual and his choice of colors as favorites or his reactions to them, may that not be a mostly personal thing? Is it so much a matter of color that makes most human beings prefer a sunny day to a rainy one as it is the physical comfort of the one and the physical discomfort of the other? If you live in a cloudless desert for even a few months you will find great excitement and beauty in a thunderstorm. Color itself can hardly be to blame.

For myself I greet color as it comes with the changing hours of the day or the slow wheel of the seasons and take great pleasure in each when it appears. And I would not like to live always in the blazing white and gold of winter nor in the violent green and blue of tropic summer; I would like some of both. Likewise in Chinese painting I would not like to live eternally in the monochrome landscape world, neither in the many-colored landscape world, but partly in both.

Certainly the world of green and blue is a lovely, lovely, lovely world. Take the Havemeyer Sea and Sky at Sunrise, which bears the name of Chao Po-chu, with its startlement of green volcanic peaks garlanded with whorls of white clouds. Pure fantasy this picture. It is a horizontal scroll, and the observer is expected to enter it at the right and to proceed to the left. If he does so he will see at once the far-off peaks of the mainland and shortly after the ascending pinnacles of a faery island. There is no inviting path to guide him through this country, no bridge

Sea and Sky at Sunrise (detail), after Chao Po-chu (*fl.* 1127–1162). Metropolitan Museum of Art.

Spring Morning at the Palaces of Han, can be considered in either category. No prettier picture ever came out of China. No prettier picture was ever painted. Squabble about authenticity, squabble about its date, he who chooses may. A few, a very few, human beings do not like to squabble under any circumstances; others like to squabble most of the time, like the English sparrow. Perhaps it is unfair to suggest that critics and curators, professors and procurers have sparrow blood, the pressure of which is often high, but it sometimes seems so, and if in the sound and fury some truth appears, there is a gain. But if in the pleasurable heat of battle one loses sight of the object one battles about, there surely is a loss. In the matter of exact attributions I grow more timid every year. Whether this picture was actually painted by Chao Po-chu or not I do not know, but I am convinced that it is of his period, the Sung dynasty. And even suppose that the blasphemous suggestion that it could be the work of a nineteenth-century snuff-bottle painter should be proved— it cannot, but if it could, what then? No talk pontifical or irresponsible can alter the intrinsic loveliness of this little picture of lakes and palaces, of blue and green hills, of exquisite people and delicately delineated shrubs and trees. It is a small picture. It is a miniature, and as the baffled Sirén says, "It may be admitted that a picture in the size of a miniature is more difficult to attribute definitely than pictures on a larger scale." Quite possibly it is too small to judge as a picture scaled to the human eye. In that case leave judgment out, enjoy it for the delicate, pretty, fragile thing it is, a hummingbird picture, the cascading trill of the Golden Bell cricket.

Certainly from these and other pictures we can get a clear idea of what green and blue painting was in the Sung dynasty.

For the Ming dynasty Ch'iu Ying is the most famous name, so common that it is almost a trade name standing for anything pretty and sweet that has a lot of color. Gradually the scores of paintings attributed to Ch'iu Ying sift out and already we are well aware of his style. There is a gay picnic party in a bamboo grove in Boston; a single lady in a bamboo coppice in the Metropolitan; and, for landscapes, Mrs. B. F. Allen's richly painted album, in which even the sky is painted in solid blue and all the rocks are edged in gold; and a snow landscape shadowed in blue, on loan to the Metropolitan Museum.

From these we may know something of the painter Ch'iu Ying and observe the development of the green and blue category as it appeared in the Ming dynasty.

We can see it again as it appeared at its best in the Ch'ing dynasty in a pair of

Entry of the First Emperor of the Han Dynasty into Kuan Chung (detail), attributed to Chao Po-chu (*fl.* 1127–1162). In the Museum of Fine Arts, Boston.

47

fans presented to the Emperor Ch'ien Lung by the head of the imperial Han Lin academy, from which all higher officials were appointed. This pair of fans is extraordinary in several ways. One could perhaps, in an excess of zeal, question their authenticity, but there is small reason to do so. In China great artists painted fans, to be sure, still do, but, like the one we have by Prince P'u Ju, they were done as souvenirs, as amusing little toys. This particular Kuan Huai pair came from the collection of one of the imperial princes as a present from hand to hand. Really it would take an elaborate, suspicious mind to consider them in any way or for any reason a hoax. These surely are paintings by Kuan Huai and with the writing of Wang Yu-tun, the head of the Han Lin academy, on the reverse—a presentation of the green and blue in its eighteenth-century phase. These fan landscapes, glittering with blue and green, are more than the surface of things. Here at long last is painting that does "probe the meaning that lies within." At this late date and in this decorative tradition we have the understanding of the great Sung masters modestly set forth in terms of blue and green. This is a surprise and contradiction to orderly cataloguing, but valid.

You might think we had done with green and blue landscapes, but no. In 1948, we had an exhibition of contemporary Chinese painting mostly "traditional" but alive and changing. Here, in 1948, we had the ramping horses of Hsu Pei-hung, the interminable but lively shrimps of Ch'i Pai-shih; contemporary shrimps, not Sung dynasty shrimps. Likewise there appeared the pale shafts of rocks and picnickers of Ho T'ien-chien and the waterfall of Wu Hu-fan. Green and blue they were, no copy of the past but lovely and a stubborn persistence of something learned long ago and never lost.

Is this not a good thing? Human beings quite rightfully boast of themselves; they are no doubt cleverer than the rest of the animal world. Their works show it even when, as lately, their architecture—*vide* Stuyvesant Town and other building projects—takes on the aspect of an ant hill. Clever indeed are human beings, but there seems to be a difference between China and the Christian West. The Chinese, learning a good principle, such as loyalty to parents and family and to the state, have until lately persisted in it. Having learned in art the pleasantness of green and blue, they still persist.

6. Other Landscapes

"I rode one evening with Count Maddalo
Upon the bank of land which breaks the flow
Of Adria towards Venice: a bare strand
Of hillocks, heaped from ever-shifting sand. . . .
This ride was my delight. I love all waste
And solitary places; where we taste
The pleasure of believing what we see
Is boundless, as we wish our souls to be."
　　　　—SHELLEY, "Julian and Maddalo"

IT IS easy for the Western eye to isolate from the huge mass of Chinese painting landscapes in monochrome and landscapes in which green and blue predominate. These attract our eye as extremes and we can catalogue them neatly. But in between the two is a long tradition of painting which has taken a middle ground—bits of color in an essentially monochrome landscape, a faint tinge of green or blue on a brown mountaintop, carefully delineated trees with red or yellow leaves—sometimes using a medley of colors. These various ways of presenting a landscape cannot be lumped together, the first might be closely linked with the monochromes and considered an offshoot, but the latter cannot be considered simply as a variation of the blue and green landscapes. There is the difference that there is in gardening, the difference between the carefully prepared beds of rich earth in which carefully spaced tiny green spears or shoots appear fresh and jewel-like, and the full richness of a summer garden where the brown earth is completely hidden. But only in the effect on the eye can this analogy be followed because in a garden the second follows naturally upon the first and in Chinese painting the one does not follow upon the other. It is a deliberate human choice, a deliberate selection on the part of the painter as he creates his landscape, a landscape of his choosing, landscape both real and fantastic.

It is like so many other things that human beings occupy themselves with. They spend a great deal of time making up rules and explanations for all sorts of things *after* the event. Right and proper that they should do so, and they have accomplished wonders. The endless avid curiosity, the passion for explaining and knowing, is a vital force which builds the world of the mind as surely as coral builds islands. But it is one thing to catalogue animals and plants and insects by inexorable natural laws, and it is quite another thing to try to catalogue the various productions of the human mind in the same way. No doubt the human mind is subject to equally inexorable laws, but we have not yet caught up with them and at the present stage the harder we try, the more often we blunder. Our attempts to deal with pictures, for instance. We make histories of paintings, their antecedents, their beginnings, their maturity, their fadings, their influences. It looks quite often like Gray's botany, but where Gray's botany is on certain ground the art historians are not. To be sure, they can record times and dates and places, all valuable to human knowledge, but they are not content with that; with a study called aesthetics (the study of beauty) they attempt to explain the past and would like to discipline the future—of beauty. Often they fool themselves into thinking that "beauty" is something tangible or concrete. We are all sure that beauty exists as we are sure of love and honor and good and evil. We have a conviction which is certainly one of the things we live by that if we can track them down these things are as hard as diamonds, as strong as Gibraltar—we believe it and probably should not laugh at the nonsense people talk about them.

And they do talk a good deal of nonsense about them, some of it boring and some of it funny—and particularly they talk nonsense about the arts, about painting, and more particularly they talk nonsense about Chinese painting. This is not to say that they do not talk a great deal of truth as well. There are many fine books on aesthetics, on the principles of design and color and the terms and definitions. Most of these are clear and intelligible reading to anyone interested in painting. "Significant form," "tactile values," "material and spiritual significance," and the others, are as meaningful now as they were when their author invented them. But they and the rest of the terminologies are only meaningful to those that have read the books. They are not as yet, and are never likely to be, part of the general public's everyday vocabulary. Proper that the profession should have a language of its own (as does medicine and the law), but I do not think it is proper to force it upon the dinner table or the ordinary communications of human beings who wish innocently to discuss pictures with one another. And it can be said that as yet the technical terminology of the arts has not arrived at any such agreement in usage as the terminology of medicine and law. The Chinese early felt this need for terminology, the sturdiest monument of which is the essay on landscape by Kuo Ssu, the son of the famous painter Kuo Hsi. The Chinese for centuries have puzzled over the exact meaning of the six principles laid down by an earlier

50

writer Hsieh Ho. Westerners have been puzzling for a scant half-century over them and loud is their disagreement as to the interpretation. The best so far is George Rowley's *Principles of Chinese Painting*, a book as valuable to the Chinese as to Westerners because it is done with a profound understanding of both Eastern and Western painting, of terminology and of philosophy. One can read it with great profit, but it is not likely to become everyday talk.

Many a Western scholar has entered the lists to translate the six principles into English, to translate literally and to translate into Western meaning.

Pray look at an attempt to translate literally:
1. Spirit resonance life movement.
2. Bone method using brush.
3. Conforming the object to a presentment of shape.
4. Follow the type in applying the colors.
5. Direct the building, place the elements.
6. Transmit and copy.

Try to approximate it in terms understandable to the Westerner:
1. It is the spirit, the rhythm, and the impression of life.
2. Good drawing—the bones of rocks and trees as well as people.
3. Plan your presentment of your object to appear real.
4. Appropriate color.
5. Take pains with composition.
6. To transmit—to continue and repeat past paintings in copies.

There is great matter here, and much to ponder upon which may well increase your pleasure in Chinese and Western pictures if you pursue it, but do not be discouraged if it seems nonsense and do not let such terminology, Chinese or Western, stand between you and the picture, Oriental or Occidental as the case may be. Paintings need not be restricted to the privileged few but are there for any man to look at and take or leave as he chooses.

While it is right and proper that a long history of Chinese painting complete with schools and influences should be written, this is not necessary for the Westerner to enjoy the Chinese paintings he comes across. Every little country inn in China, every roadside temple, has pictures which every illiterate Chinese farmer enjoys. For centuries there has been a trickle at least of Chinese art into the Occident—by the eighteenth century the trickle had increased to a flow, in the last fifty years it has become almost a deluge. Find me a hamlet in the United States where there is not at least one Chinese picture even though it be only a rice-paper set of "mandarins" or tortures. Remember, almost every educated Chinese boy or girl paints and is apt to paint prettily if not well. The modern Chinese painters are haughty and self-conscious (they have caught it from us) and apt to demand high prices, but you have only to go through the antique shops on the avenues or watch the auction houses to realize that in our day there is almost as much Chinese painting about as there is in China. "Deluge" is not an extravagant word to use for it.

This means, if nothing else, that the American eye is growing accustomed to Chinese painting; and while it is a rare thing for a masterpiece to turn up in a lowly antique shop, quite often a charming and remote reflection of one does. Do not despise them. The late Denman Ross, gentle, ponderous, dewlapped, rheumy-eyed like a benevolent St. Bernard, was wont to sigh and say, "This is not a great picture, but it is the formula—the formula is good." Bernard Berenson once rebuked a rash Harvard student who had remarked that the business of Chinese painting was sometimes wearying—one must look at five hundred or a thousand second- and third-rate Chinese paintings to find a first-rate one. "Yes!" snapped Mr. Berenson, "but never forget that the tenth-rate one is first-rate."

While it is true that objects of Chinese art have been brought to the West for centuries, they were mostly porcelains, lacquers, the brightly decorated papers of the tea boxes. Not until after the mid-nineteenth century did the West become aware of formal Chinese painting. Our interest and knowledge increases apace, but the early interpretive books have not yet been displaced, and any one would do well to read Fenollosa's *Epochs of Chinese and Japanese Art*, Binyon's *Flight of the Dragon* and *Painting in the Far East*, Arthur Waley's *An Introduction to the Study of Chinese Painting*, and Petrucci's *Chinese Painting*. This generation may be much wiser, but as yet they have not written so understandingly or well.

All the early books consider the great period of Chinese painting at an end with the Yuan period (1280–1368) and speak of later painting slightingly if at all. Recently champions of Ming and Ch'ing painting have appeared, vociferous in their praise of later painting and often scornful of the early periods.

There is really no need for controversy in this matter at all. Let each man select what he likes best. The historians of Western art have worked out a pattern that is quite successful for Western painting particularly since the Renaissance. Giotto and Duccio, breaking away from the hieratic religious painting of Byzantium, become "primitives," and one can trace the rapid development to Titian and Michelangelo and watch them, having achieved that glory, fade away. Western painting resolves itself easily into schools and comparatively brief periods of time. The student of Chinese painting is faced with two thousand years and more of a tradition of painting which, although it has been refreshed from time to time by outside influences and undergone changes within itself, has never deserted its original principles. It starts with outline and flat colors—it has developed a marvelous variation of outline by means of brushes so that an outline becomes almost a wash. It has developed intricacies of composition and design, but it has never been diverted by experiment or technique as Western painting has. This is not to say that one is better than another, but simply that this is so. Perspective as such has not interested the Chinese much—Castiglione caused scarcely a ripple. The Chinese achieved a way of informing the eye of distance by placing things near at the bottom of a painting, placing things far at the top of a picture, and leaving spaces in between, or they painted as if they were sitting on a hilltop looking down on the scene below. This often gives the observer the impression of perspective projection, which it is not. It is sometimes called a geometric or isometric projection, which is a distinct method of expression in its own right and which has definite advantage over perspective rendering.

As Mr. Arthur Pope of Harvard University says in his second volume of *Introduction to the Language of Drawing and Painting*, "In Chinese and Japanese painting, and in mediaeval and much other painting of the West, there is often no pretense of rendering the superficial appearance of things to the eye; nevertheless there may be a perfectly clear expression of the essential character of things."

His footnote on perspective seems worth quoting in full: "At the present day we are used to perspective renderings, partly because the camera gives us perspective renderings, but this is more or less of an accident. If the camera gave us isometric instead of perspective projections, we might think of this other kind of rendering as just as natural and understandable as perspective. No one ever stops to think that a photograph, as we ordinarily look at it, is inaccurate; but it really is, for in looking at a photograph we can almost never get our eye near enough to the picture to make it correspond exactly to a true image on the retina of the eye. At the same time many people think of a photograph taken with the camera tilted in such a way that the vertical lines of buildings converge diagonally as a distortion, just because they are used to vertical plane and not to inclined plane perspective; but as a matter of fact one is just as accurate—or as inaccurate—as the other." The Chinese bothered very little about perspective and very little about three-dimensional modeling or the light and shade we call chiaroscuro. These things did not interest them.

The Chinese like their way of making pictures and they have been at it a very long time. If we apply the pattern we have worked out for Western schools of painting, then most would agree that Chinese painting reached its most majestic heights in T'ang (618–906) and Sung (960–1280) painting; but they had left much undone, and it is not fair to say that the painting of succeeding centuries is a mere fading away. The Ming and Ch'ing dynasties had many great painters who discovered many new and fresh ways of saying things. The contemporary exhibition shown at the Metropolitan Museum in 1948 proved that they are still at it.

River for an Elder Brother (detail), attributed to Ch'en Tao-fu (1483–1544). Metropolitan Museum of Art.

There is really nothing for people to quarrel about in this. It is like books or poems—you may wish to read one one day and another the next. There is a long horizontal scroll of bamboos in the Fogg Museum of Harvard attributed to Chin-wen-chin. To look at this is like spending a day on a river in a forest of bamboos. As the scroll unrolls you see sometimes groves of trees complete, sometimes merely wind-tossed tops, sometimes the trunks as they emerge from the ground. There is a horizontal scroll of lotus flowers attributed to Ch'en Hsun (also known as Ch'en Tao-fu) in the William Rockhill Nelson Museum in Kansas City which is as good as a July day on the North, the Middle, and the South seas, which is the name given to the three artificial lakes of the Imperial garden palaces of Peking. There is the river scroll called River for an Elder Brother attributed to Ch'en Tao-fu in the Metropolitan Museum. To look at this landscape is as refreshing as to spend a long and perfect day in the country. There are no snares or pitfalls in it, no plagues of noxious insects or unwelcome picnickers in a favorite spot. It presents, I should say, a day in September—a day of delicious temperature, warm enough to raise a delicate haze on distant flats and mountains, but not too warm to walk in—a day with light breezes that propel occasional sails, suggesting the pleasant alternative of taking a boat if one is not disposed to walk. The sun falls pale and white upon the river. The water flows quiet and serene; only once, when momentarily confined by an arched bridge, does it break into rapid movement. The country through which the river runs is varied and pleasant; though fairly wild and rugged at times, it is never grandiose or terrifying.

54

River for an Elder Brother (detail), attributed to Ch'en Tao-fu (1483–1544). Metropolitan Museum of Art.

At the beginning of the scroll the observer finds himself upon a promontory with a few houses and a bridge from which he looks across the wideness of the river to the far bank and lowlands. For some distance—a mile, two miles perhaps —he proceeds through narrows, past occasional small villages and temples and rather fine rocks, meeting occasional strollers and catching sight of two or three sailboats, an island, groups of trees, reeds. Then he discovers a distant mountain range, rising from plain to foothill, from foothill to peak. In the course of the river day he passes two such ranges and finally, at the end of it, comes again to flat lowland, to open water with little boats in the distance, and at the very last to nothing at all. From this most pleasant state of being, the observer is snapped back into the world he has lately left by a brief burst of sky-written calligraphy in which the painter signs off with two of his intimate names or nicknames, "White Shining Mountain Man" and "Follower of the Way" (Tao), and explains that the scroll was painted "in play" for an elder brother. This is the river trip and the kind of day which Ch'en Tao-fu offers to anyone who cares to look.

The technique of the river scroll would certainly have outraged the painter of The Tribute Horse, and it is likely to annoy and exasperate any right-thinking realist. If, however, one remembers that the picture was painted in play he will be more amused than offended at the visual tricks—and there are a good many— that the artist has played on him. In the first place, very few colors are used throughout the scroll: neutralized yellow, orange that is almost a faded tiger color, grayish blue that is sometimes greenish and that is occasionally strengthened in intensity on a distant mountain peak, and a great deal of gray. Having set forth these subdued, autumnal, pastel hues, Ch'en Tao-fu makes them the background for a bravura performance of electric black brush strokes with which he directs attention to the shapes of foreground rocks and sails, an occasional wayfarer, temples, reeds, and trees. This brush-stroke performance is brilliant in the extreme. If one blinks slightly on finding that a fisherman walking across a bridge in the middle ground is four times the size of the men in sailboats in the foreground, or on discovering that tiny lichens and plant forms, which according to the classical convention should be represented as tiny dots, have here been exaggerated into loud, staccato arpeggios, it is not hard to forgive the painter. This is a minor license when one takes into consideration the successful illusion of the painting as a whole and the almost countless details which, flashed in with dazzling speed and brevity, delight the eye with the sheer brilliance of their execution. There is a passage of water reeds, a congregation of sails behind a rock, a tier of distant mountain peaks—many such things—that can hardly be equaled in any painting we know.

7. Spring Festival on the River

Ch'ing Ming, which literally means "clear and bright," is the name given in China to the spring festival dedicated to the honorably buried dead. (A summer festival is dedicated to lost souls and hungry ghosts, those who have died without families to honor them, those whose bodies have been lost in battle or at sea, and those so sad and desperate that they have destroyed themselves.) The festival of Ch'ing Ming is variable in date, coming one hundred and six days after the winter solstice. In the Chinese calendar this occurs early in the third moon or late in the second, usually late March or early April.

It is likely that this festival originated in or takes the place of one of those primitive prehistoric celebrations of life-renewal so dear to those scholars whose great desire seems to be to swing once more upon the Golden Bough. One of the customs associated with it is the planting of trees, and it is sometimes called *Chih Shu Chieh*, or "Tree-Planting Festival." In this respect it is a Chinese version of Arbor Day. Whatever its origins, however, the Ch'ing Ming long ago became a Chinese version of All Saints' Day or the American Memorial Day. The symbol hunters, so eager-terrier-eyed in their chase for origins (which almost always arrive at ♂ or ♀), forget that symbols may grow up and become something completely different from what they started out to be. It seems better, therefore, to understand what the Ch'ing Ming now is than what it once was. The sole purpose of the Ch'ing Ming nowadays is to honor one's family dead, a custom reverent and civilized.

As celebrated in twentieth century China this festival is a day when many people visit their family graves, to decorate them with prayers written in black ink on white paper and with wands of willow. In the country it is a pretty sight to see—

the bright sun shining on the lion-colored hills, the tawny fields, the delicate, sparse tracery of green, and the countless family processions moving in every direction to and fro across the countryside. The families march in single file, usually with the eldest and tallest in front and the children in decreasing size bringing up the rear. All are dressed in garments which may, when the cloth was dyed, have been a consistent, hard aniline ultramarine blue but which, when washed and faded, have turned into a great variety of blues—indigo, gentian, delphinium, morning glory, and robin's egg. Aside from the ceremonies at the graves, there are feasts and shows and entertainments of every kind for the living.

It is with this latter aspect of the festival that the painting of the Ch'ing Ming on which we are at work is concerned. In fact, in the picture itself there is no hint at all of the purpose of the festival—no tombs, no mounds, no willow wands, no paper prayers; that part must be taken for granted as a ceremony completed, so that the observer may give full attention to the worldly business of the day.

The subject was first ordered by the Emperor Hui Tsung of the Sung dynasty (960–1279) about 1120 from the painter Chang Tse-tuan. The picture was called, and all copies and later versions have been called after it, Ch'ing Ming Shang Ho ("Spring Festival on the River"). It is the painter's representation of a spring festival day in and about a city on the Yellow River. His model would be, of course, the Sung capital Pien Ching (the present-day K'ai Feng). The painting, however, must not be mistaken for an accurate panorama of either the city or the river. But, on the other hand, in its myriad detail it gives a very accurate picture of the life and city of its period, and this is true also of later copies, which, though they may slip into anachronistic detail here and there, on the whole follow the original closely.

In this seeming contradiction—it is not accurate; it is very accurate—lies one of the fundamental concepts of Chinese painting, the spirit, or *ch'i*. Take, for instance, the palace scenes: they are not exact as an architect's drawing pretends to be, but they look far more like the real thing than any such drawing or a photograph. This is what is meant by *ch'i*—the very breath and soul of a thing. Our Western critics get a dusty inkling of the idea when they speak lightly of a "spirited" sketch.

The Museum's version of this painting, which is from the famous collection of A. W. Bahr, was made early in the Ming dynasty (1368–1644). It is optimistically inscribed with the name of the painter Ch'iu Ying, who was active from about 1522 to 1560, but the signature is of interest only because it is recorded that Ch'iu Ying did a version. As painting the picture is the work of a very creditable Ming painter following the traditional style.

It is the amazing content of this work which is its chief interest. The artist has made, in a single scroll, an extraordinarily complete pictorial record of life in

58

Spring Festival on the River, Ming Dynasty version of a Sung Dynasty painting by Chang Tse-tuan. Ex coll. Bahr, Metropolitan Museum of Art.

medieval China. The historian with all available data at hand, if he wishes to make a picture of a particular time, must reconstruct it from fragments of pictures and bits of written description. In this instance—and so far as I know the work has no parallel in the pictorial records of other civilizations—almost everything that the historian wants to see is here. Here, first of all, are the people of China as they have lived for many centuries and much as they were still living at the beginning of the twentieth century. Life in China as late as 1935 had so much that was like what one sees in this picture that one knows that most of the details are true and believes in the rest.

To begin with, the natural background, the river itself, and the highly colored hills are recognizable, not as in a colored photograph, but in their essential character. So also are the little towns and the great city.

Walls such as we see in the painting still exist. Most magnificent among them are those of Sianfu, in Shensi, and Peking. The walls of Sian, which was the T'ang capital, are rather stern and bleak; the walls of the present Peking are on a mightier but more gracious scale (if one has seen Peking one is sure of the rightness of the walls in the painting). As for the streets and the shops, one may see them in city after city. Palaces not too dissimilar also remain, but the people who lived in them in very recent years have either vanished from the scene or withdrawn to a less gorgeous mode of life.

Most of the various types of people represented, as has been said, are still to be seen in China, bent on the same activities but in clothes much modified and changed. Here in the painting are the people of China in almost every walk of life: beggars, mendicants, farmers, goat-herds, peddlers, shopkeepers of small shops and great, restaurateurs, jugglers, actors, fortunetellers (note the number of these), doctors, innkeepers, teachers, officials (synonymous with scholars in ancient China)—officials small, officials great, officials poor, officials rich—and children, mostly little boys in a diversity of harmless mischief. Here they all are and also their activities.

There are shops of every kind to be seen here: wine shops, a grain market, secondhand shops, crockery shops, bow and arrow shops, lantern shops, a lute-making shop, a gold and silver ornament shop, a dyeing shop, picture shops, a medicine shop, pawnshops, a needle shop, antique shops, restaurants, and more. And not only shops but trades and occupations: millers and metalworkers, carpenters and masons; and the means of transport: river boats and large wheeled wagons, some with an eight-mule hitch, coolies with panniers suspended from poles, donkeys and mules, parade horses and palfreys, sedan chairs and princely chariots, plebeian ferries and aristocratic houseboats—all are here.

As to the manner and style of representation, much may be said. The work may be tagged, if one likes, as an academic painting in the blue and green landscape tradition, which dates back as far as the T'ang dynasty (618–907) and has persisted, subject to changes in fashion, until the present day. Its style is delightful in color and capable of many moods—in this case, a mood almost entirely gay and festive, executed by an extremely competent painter. In its interest in crowds and parades it makes one think a little of Jacques Callot or Gentile Bellini and now and then of Carpaccio, but their crowds and processions are confined to a composition rectangular and static, whereas this one goes on and on with the illusion of movement.

Comparisons are not necessarily odious, but they are generally frowned upon—especially when different kinds of sensory experience are involved. (We have five senses and supposedly only one mind.) Those who set up to be critics of the arts, it would seem, do not allow such comparisons. In this most people support them.

Spring Festival on the River, Ming Dynasty version of a Sung Dynasty painting by Chang Tse-tuan. Ex coll. Bahr, Metropolitan Museum of Art.

Most people object to being told that a rose smells pink or that Debussy's music sounds mostly blue and green or that Renoir's brush strokes are luscious, succulent. Most people take their five senses seriously and separately; they do not like to have them mixed. While this is true, writer after writer dealing with Chinese painting falls into a way of speaking of it—particularly in the horizontal scrolls—as if it were a piece of music. The writers apologize, but they do so. They would better come to terms.

Music moves; on the ear it moves and is never at rest. Westerners have a way of recording music for the eye, and musicians can read a piece of music; the mind of the Westerner, informed by his eye, knows what his ear should hear—isn't that so? Very well. In the long Chinese scrolls—the Ch'ing Ming, for instance, there is a likeness to music which we can describe.

If we analyze the Ch'ing Ming we will find that in its thirty-three feet it plays themes just as a piece of music does. The Ch'ing Ming, of course, is no symphony, no sonata; it is an elaborate tone poem. Its themes and subjects are not static; they change. They begin, develop, and are neatly finished off, as they would be in good music. The themes, while remaining independent entities, balance and interweave.

The subject of the painting is, first of all, a spring festival; the holiday spirit is implicit throughout the composition. There are some thirty-three feet of this composition, but the effect is of some thirty-three miles. It is not a panorama, a bird's-eye view; it is a kind of moving picture at which the spectator does the moving and has the advantage of being able to turn forward or back.

In this scroll, as in almost all landscape scrolls, there is a road for the spectator to follow. This almost goes without saying—so much so that one could easily forget that it is the road (the first theme) which carries one all the way through; in this case, a country road which soon joins the river (the second theme) and increases in importance until the climax of road and river is reached at the bridge, which is the busiest of market places. The road continues as a city street, almost—but not quite—drops out of sight as it passes the military display, proceeds by the hunting party and village scenes, and vanishes at the end with the air of a road that has put in a full day but can go on forever.

The river, the second theme, appears almost at once, increases in importance for nearly a third of the picture, continues as small canals and tributaries for the second third, and vanishes behind mountains until almost the end, where road and river meet again as part of a country landscape. The road and the river are the background for the more spectacular themes of the scroll.

Like the road, the holiday crowd (the third theme) follows from beginning to end. Like the road, people, moving mostly from right to left, increase in numbers and activity up to the bridge scene, are prominent in the city street, shrink to a few passers-by outside the military scene, leisurely take prominence again in the hunting party and village scenes, and diminish at the end of the picture. It is by intention, for balance, that the movement of human life in the picture is from right to left, while the movement of the river, as may be seen in the way the coolies pull and row, is from left to right.

The road, the river, and men on holiday are the major themes of the picture. They are there at the beginning, fresh at dawn; they are there at the end, tired but tranquil at dusk.

It is a question whether to call the fourth theme architecture or to break it into several. Like the first three, and more impressive, it is always there; but different aspects are so emphasized that it seems clearer to subdivide it.

Dwellings there are from one end to the other of the painting—every conceivable

Spring Festival on the River, Ming Dynasty version of a Sung Dynasty painting by Chang Tse-tuan. Ex coll. Bahr, Metropolitan Museum of Art.

kind from country farm to city house, mansion, palace, and back at last to country farmhouse again.

If we break the theme of architecture, the shops (which are, of course, closely associated with the road and the city street) can be counted as a fifth theme, which begins as we reach the suburbs of the city, continues—after the bridge and river climax—importantly through the city, and recurs here and there until the end.

Sixth is the city walls and gates, with the magnificent pavilions or towers which surmount the gates. These appear twice, and in actual space comparatively briefly, but are most important. In the music of brick and wall they tower up with a triumphal splendor that is akin to that of the more splendid passages of Wagner's *Parsifal*. If the bridge and market scene is the peak of the crescendo of the road, the river, and men on holiday, the walls are a majestic statement of what men can build. Their first appearance marks approximately the first third of the scroll.

Inside the walls we come upon the grandeurs of the city. At the far end the walls appear again, repeating ever more splendidly the theme. This occurs at not quite the second third of the scroll.

Inside the walls is a splendid street with shops and residences, one a palace. The palace is part of the theme of architecture; yet, like the walls, it should be counted as a separate theme (the seventh). To all intents and purposes it is a royal palace. If we consider the theme of dwelling places, it is to this that it has been building up; it is from this that it will gently diminish. The palace is part of a larger scheme and also a thing in itself—a pretty thing like a Debussy *Arabesque*.

The eighth theme, roof lines, is properly only a part of the preceding themes, but it is in the repetition of the developed pattern of roof lines that one can see most clearly the way the painter composed his scroll. The roof lines, if one could wash everything else out of the picture, would present an entrancing composition by themselves. Reduced to simplest terms, they are but brief, straight lines of varying length, punctuated at the ends. But they are as alive as dragonflies and, like dragonflies over a summer pond, they appear first two or three at a time and then in increasing crowds with a multiplicity of direction. Could one freeze a dragonfly ballet one might get something like the pattern of these roofs, save that the roofs are deliberately arranged and purposeful. In this picture we are aware of the roofs and their pattern. Something a little like it could be seen in New York several years ago when the lights were blacked out and the moon outlined our very different roofs and towers, roofs and towers which ordinarily we forget. In such great cities as Sian and Lanchow the roofs and walls are nightly in evidence and for a period each month are illumined by the moon.

When we reach the third part of the picture, a theme seemingly new is introduced—a grand military display (a parade is part of any proper holiday). It is not really new. Just as the palace was a culmination of the dwelling places, just as men at the bridge reached a full tide of human busyness, the military display is a statement of human activity as seen in official holiday spectacle. It becomes a special thing, almost an independent interlude. The gateways of the government buildings have been turned into reviewing stands; before them is the field, where platoons of troops with banners frame a kind of gymkhana with competitions in archery, swordsmanship, and riding.

The simpler versions of the scroll, which probably follow the original more closely than ours does, move from a brief military display back to the river and a pageant of festival boats. Our painting makes much of the army festival, omits entirely the elaborate dragon and feng huang boats, and substitutes instead a royal hunt in miniature. One can only guess at the reason, but one can make a good

Spring Festival on the River, Ming Dynasty version of a Sung Dynasty painting by Chang Tse-tuan. Ex coll. Bahr, Metropolitan Museum of Art.

guess: hunting scenes became popular in the Yuan dynasty (1280–1368), for one thing. Peking, which became the Ming capital in 1421, has canals and pretty artificial lakes, but northern China, while it has waterways and boats, did not make so much of them as southern China. At any rate the painter of our scroll, although he has multiplied the commercial boats and tucked in one official boat (which resembles the boats used even today on the palace lakes), has omitted the pageant of festival boats entirely.

The hunt which takes the place of the water pageant is a beauty. It has all the aspects of a royal hunt but is, like the palace scenes, carefully anonymous. We come upon it, as we follow the scroll, just as we came upon the palace itself and the military function, by the back door; so we see the most important part of the progress to the hunting field first. Leaving the city is a merry party, a Chinese version of those described in the *Morte d'Arthur*. In it are two chariots of elegance, one occupied by two beauties with a cavalcade of female riders, the other by an official dressed in brilliant red. Preceding them is a numerous escort of mounted warriors, grooms, footmen, and flag-bearers. The procession leaves the highroad and twists back and forth through mountains (all in the actual space of a few inches) until it arrives at a remote hunting ground where great silk pavilions have been set up for the hunting party. These tents are gorgeous—gorgeous in the painting and even more gorgeous in fact. Beyond the tents appear glimpses of the hunters themselves, riding armed with spears in pursuit of a tiger, foxes, deer, and scurrying small animals. We must count the hunting party, although less relevant than the missing boat festival, as a tenth theme in the scroll.

The eleventh theme, however, the mountains in which the hunt is set, can be regarded as one of the background motives. They appear at the very beginning of the scroll, come into prominence, vanish at the outskirts of the city, reappear after the gymkhana, and continue to the end, where in quiet, solid masses, like a series of great chords in a musical finale, they conclude the movement of the picture—but not until they have diminished from the hunting scene and become background for a village or two and a very handsome birthday party for an ancient scholar and his wife.

At the very end of the scroll the action quiets down. As at the beginning we are in the country, this time at the end of the day; here are hills again, rice fields, and a relaxed supper party at a farm or country house with a tired, languid dog picking up scraps.

The birthday party surely would count, not as a major theme, but merely as a minor variation or extra decoration. There are many such diversions through the picture, and they are often used to mark a transition from one major theme to another. The various temples that appear are cunningly placed to act as pauses. There are also scenes in miniature that are reminders of famous paintings—the bathing horses of Chao Meng-fu, the playing horses of Han Kan, for instance, which are tucked in outside the city walls. From one end of the scroll to the other the painter has included bits of reminiscence.

It is a very ambitious thing for any painter to attempt to record the whole world in a single picture, but the painter of our spring festival has recorded the world he knew in a picture which not only turns out to be an invaluable human document (as good in its way as S. Wells Williams's *The Middle Kingdom*) but which has in its conception as a work of art the bones and sinews of a great tradition of painting. Analyze it as we please, before we begin and when we are done, this picture is a song of a whole people tuned to a holiday—a holiday called Clear and Bright—who move from dawn till dusk along a river and a road.

8. Play with Infants

"Heaven lies about us in our infancy!
  Shades of the prison-house
  Begin to close
  Upon the growing Boy,
  But he beholds the light, and whence it flows,
  He sees it in his joy."
        —WILLIAM WORDSWORTH,
     "Ode on Intimations of Immortality"

CHOU FANG was a painter of great fame during the last years of the eighth century, and his fame, far from diminishing, has increased in luster ever since. One painting attributed to him is called Play with Infants and depicts a group of kindly mothers with their young. It is a small picture, only twelve inches high and twenty inches in width, perhaps a fragment of a longer horizontal scroll, perhaps complete as it is. It bears a number of seals and colophons which have the appearance of integrity.

Although attributed to Chou Fang in handling and performance, it belongs with a group of paintings generally called by Western students Five Dynasties (907–960) and early Sung. It may be compared to the Chess Players in the Freer Gallery in Washington and to the Silk Makers in the Museum of Fine Arts in Boston associated with Hui Tsung (likewise once attributed to Chou Fang).

The second inscription on Play with Infants is an essay-poem signed by Ko Ch'i (1336–1374) which has been freely translated by Han Shou-hsuan as follows:

"Near the windblown fence which surrounds the peonies and beside the open well which is close by *wu tung* trees, delicate infants are engaged in afternoon play while young ladies are comparing their spring dresses. The children are all surprised to learn that pearls come from oysters and jade from rock.

"The infants are partially dressed in swaddling clothes of variegated brocade. They wear purple gauze bags obliquely. Their dripping bangs are short. They will grow to be the fine sons in front of Wang's hall and those of Wei on the road. Their bodies sprawl comfortably on soft grass; their hands toy with fragrant

67

Play with Infants, attributed to Chou Fang (eighth century). Metropolitan Museum of Art.

flowers. Each of them is eager to play with someone. One is hiding himself to elude the others; another is prevented from catching painted butterflies; one is encouraged to play with a wax feng huang bird; another is being dusted with talcum powder, while still another is taking a bath scented with aloe wood.

"These infants are the equals of that famous son who was a stone unicorn in heaven and was then sent to earth in the house of Minister Hsu and of the renowned nephews who grew up in the halls of the Prime Minister Hsien.

"They all look equally attractive because they are all equally loved. Their ages appear to be the same, and it is difficult to decide which are the older ones.

"It is hard for you to match him who has sons, but your daughters are enough to make up a line.

"My affectionate sympathy on your acquiring this painting. Truly it is a good omen of dream bears."

As often this poem is full of literary references. Those who read Chinese, including Chinese scholars themselves, are fond of saying Chinese poetry cannot be translated. It can be in the most important matter, which is the poetic idea and which can be released from whatever rigid form it may be imprisoned in. It is interesting to know that in the fourth century the sons of the Wang family were

68

Play with Infants (detail), attributed to Chou Fang (eighth century). Metropolitan Museum of Art.

so famous that people liked to go to the Wang family to select their sons-in-law and that Wei Chieh (286–312) was so handsome that when he went out "on the road" a crowd usually surrounded him. In addition, the reference to dream bears needs a little explaining. The bear is a symbol of a brave warrior. To dream of one is a good omen of having sons.

Aside from this there is much matter in this poem. Kao Ch'i describes all sorts of things that no physical eye can see. In the actual picture there are no fences, no grass, no peonies, no *wu tung* tree. If there ever was a butterfly, it has fluttered its ephemeral wings and vanished. Yet every observer knows these infants and women are out of doors and that it is the summer season. Why? There is not the slightest indication except, perhaps, the lack of indoor furniture and the extreme *décolleté* and *déjambé* of the infants. Kao Ch'i knew it was out of doors, and quite unconsciously in his description he supplies the peonies and *wu tung* trees which, of course, are close about. They must be in a garden of a great house in China.

Indeed, there is in this casual and quaint commentary of Kao Ch'i, written some six hundred years ago, something more than a clue to the happy, gentle, and serene character of the whole Chinese race as we know them today. "They all look equally attractive because they are all equally loved." There is the answer—happy babies—happy children—happy children—happy men and women. In America few children, of course, are lucky enough to be fairly well treated ("spoiled," it is generally called), but when I observe the Spartan discipline to which my friends subject their helpless but (praise be) protesting babes, I am tempted to start a campaign. My friends go to considerable trouble to get babies—they even adopt them—but once having got them they proceed to subject them to a regimen un-hampered, nay encouraged, even by societies for the prevention of cruelty to children, which no grownup outside a concentration camp would put up with for a moment. They are forcibly fed when they do not want to eat; they are consigned to solitary confinement when they do not want to sleep; and when they scream to high heaven in anguish their placid mamas say that it is good for their lungs.

Is it possible that as a people we are convinced that life at best is a horrid business and feel that we should start making our children miserable at the earliest possible moment? Consider that presentment and then look upon Chou Fang's entrancing babes. Chinese mothers approach the baby problem differently. Never is a Chinese baby left alone. If he yells, it is assumed, quite properly, that he wants something. If he wants something he should not have, he is diverted with something harmless. If he is hungry, he eats; if he is sleepy, he sleeps. And for him there are no such conventions as we drag our children through. There is no set period of babyhood, of childhood, of adolescence, with all the special attributes and conventions we make for these periods. No indeed. Your Chinese babe is always with grownups.

70

Gathering of Scholars at the Western Garden, attributed to
Chao Meng-fu(1254–1322). Metropolitan Museum of Art.

At the earliest moment he wears clothes cut like his father's clothes; he learns to use manners which his father uses. (What American child has not glared to see his paternal parent allowed to put his elbows on the table while he must sit demure?) The Chinese child instantly takes his place in the social scheme and is not always being faced with leaps and hurdles. Does this not seem more sensible?

Occasionally an earnest mother disagrees with me and talks of infant mortality and such. There does seem to be a difference on that score. I cannot deny that more American babies seem to survive; but if there were a way to measure the percentage of happy men and women, I am willing to wager that there would be a goodly margin on the Chinese side. And there is no doubt in my mind at all as to which system the babies would choose.

Most travelers and many writers have remarked on the affection lavished upon children in the Far East. The Chinese adore children and are not afraid of spoiling them—they learn etiquette and good manners more by imitation than by instruction. They rarely get beaten until they are grown up—fourteen or so, and then if they misbehave they get a good whaling, most likely by their grandmamas.

The Chinese are kind to their children and doubly kind to old people. Every year you add in China is a kind of social security much more dependable than ours. It is in the years of physical strength and emotional maturity that the Chinese bear the responsibilities of family and state. This is very different from the American way of life—and from the Soviet—to both of which the poor Chinese have been forcibly exposed over the last hundred years.

When I write of China and seem to write of the past, as my young friends both East and West most eagerly tell me, I am confident that I write of a pattern of culture that has been so successful that it cannot be destroyed and that if it should seem to in the near future it will eventually be recovered again.

"All children want to kill their parents," remarked one of my young Chinese friends who I felt had taken up Freud and his followers with too much enthusiasm. "All children want to kill their parents and in China they seem to be doing it in a big way just now." He laughed. "But this does have to stop somewhere, you know. We have very big families in China. Sooner or later somebody will stop to think. After we kill off all the old ones—who comes next?"

This is a bloodthirsty contemporary version of one of the stories of the Twenty-four Paragons of Filial Piety which for some two millenniums have been taught to Chinese children. The stories of the paragon all have some ethical precept usually advantageous to elders and are used a good deal as we use the story of George Washington and the hatchet—a story which amuses any child because it is a tale of agreeable naughtiness from which the boy escapes by pulling the virtue of truthfulness like a rabbit out of a hat.

72

Gathering of Scholars at the Western Garden (detail), attributed to Chao Meng-fu (1254–1322). Foreground: Mi Fei, Wang Chung-chih', unidentified scholar. Background: Chen Pi-shu, Chin Kuan.

The paragon relevant here is little Yuan Ku. It was a time of famine, and after much sorrow and thought it was decided to take Grandfather to the countryside and leave him to perish, for it meant one less mouth to feed. It was done. He was transported on a wooden sled and left upon a knoll. With bowed head his son—the father of the paragon—went slowly back to town. Deep in unhappy thought he became aware of a rasping sound. His little son was dragging the sled along. "Yuan Ku," the father said, "we no longer need the sled." To this the pert paragon replied, "Oh, yes, Papa, I will need it when the time comes to drag you to the country."

At this the father, member of the middle generation, burst into tears, and rushed back to rescue his parent. Whether the whole family starved or survived we are not told, but the principle is right either way.

The paragons are so well known that they are almost forgotten, and to read their stories you must hunt around in books of symbolism or legend. They are well worth hunting for, and include Lao Lai-tze, the high official, who at the age of seventy performed childish antics so that his parents would still feel young; Yen Tze who in order to get doe's milk for his mother disguised himself in a deer skin; and Ting Lan whose mother's statue scowled when beaten by a neighbor and wept when her son was jailed for punishing the offender.

And all the rest.

What happened to the children of Chou Fang's painting when they grew up? Those responsible middle years? There we have official histories—we have poems and letters, and we have paintings. Countless paintings. In them we see a way of living that seems a kind of fairy story—we see scholars contemplating the immortal hills, beauties sitting alone, the Hundred Beauties in seeming impossible palaces, scenes of pomp and ceremony and of war. Cloud Cuckoo Land? Fantasy? No. They lived that way until quite recently, and even now, stripped of the glitter and the gold which appear in the paintings, beset by political troubles at home or driven into exile, they live in their inner lives as do the people of the paintings. It is a way of life—a pattern of culture. What our eyes can see, the physical trappings, has been swept aside. What our eyes cannot see, the inner confidence in what is right and wrong, in responsibility to one's family, in good manners, persists and is likely to prove stronger than the powerful but unnatural forces which seek to destroy it.

We can see in countless pictures how the Chou Fang babies lived when they were grown up. Mostly they are anonymous or, when they have names of sages or emperors, they are so remote from us as to seem so. A handy exception to this is a painting of a garden party in the Metropolitan Museum. This garden party took place in A.D. 1087, long before there were cameras or society magazines, but

74

Gathering of Scholars at the Western Garden (detail), attributed to Chao Meng-fu (1254–1322). Seated left to right: Li Chih-yi, Su Tung-po, Tsai Tien-chi, Prince Wang Hsien.

one of the guests, himself a famous painter, made a pictorial record which was copied again and again. One copy of it attributed to Chao Meng-fu (1254–1322) was in the Chinese Imperial Collection, and is now in the possession of the Chinese National Government. The Metropolitan picture is a still later copy, probably from the early part of the Ming dynasty (1368–1644). It was long considered a pleasant garden scene until Lin Yu-tang, in the course of his research for *The Gay Genius—The Life and Times of Su Tung-po,* discovered it.

Instantly this garden party of almost nine hundred years ago becomes as intimate as the photographs in the feature of a contemporary picture magazine called "Life Goes to a Party."

In 1087 it was a very distinguished party. It took place in the garden of Prince Wang Hsien who was the emperor's brother. No less than sixteen of the great scholars of the day attended. (All sixteen appear in the Government picture—three have dropped out of the Metropolitan version.) Sixteen great scholars were there, but you must not think they were invited for a formal meeting, a public symposium or university bicentennial as they are in our contemporary scene. They were invited informally to eat and drink. Drink is not frowned upon in the Far East—rather the contrary. At such a party, just as we in our day may indulge in after-dinner games like charades or word games, so did they. One or another might dash off a poem or a sketch, and the others add their names for a souvenir. Such a thing if preserved may become an important footnote to the history of the times. So it was with this party. An impressive party anywhere. Li Lung-mien made a formal painting of it, and another painter, Mi Fei, described it fully. Three of the great painters of the Sung dynasty were there—Li Lung-mien, Mi Fei, and Su Tung-po. Su Tung-po's brother was there with his four followers.

With this information what seems to be a pretty garden picture with anonymous figures becomes a personal document. We know all their names. At the table in the foreground sits Su Tung-po himself, brush in hand, with the Prince Wang Hsien and others (Li Chih-yi, Prince Wang's lesser consorts, and Tsai Tien-chi) watching him. At the next table sits Li Lung-mien similarly occupied with his friends (Chang Lei, Huang Ting-chien, and Su Tse-yu) watching him. In the upper reaches of the garden Mi Fei in profile is busy inscribing characters upon a rock while beyond him Chin Kuan listens to a lute player.

Here are your Chou Fang children, or others like them, grown up.

Here they are and with famous names attached, no longer gentle, anonymous figures in a garden. Are they actual likenesses? It would be hard to find a subject in which there is a wider divergence of taste or a greater diversity of opinion than in portraiture, and this though the counterfeit be limned by human hand or mechanically arrived at by cutting out a silhouette or clicking the shutters of a camera. So many elements are involved, and these are often inharmonious and often strongly opposed. In most categories of painting and sculpture only two people are concerned, the maker and the observer; in portraiture a third personality obtrudes itself, that of the person painted, and there arises the emotional conflict popularly referred to as a triangle. I have noticed that there is a vast difference if the subject is oneself, or when the person depicted is a known contemporary, a relative, a friend, an acquaintance, or a person cordially disliked. Then our first-hand judgment of the sitter enters in and the conflict develops into violence. Only when we come to unnamed sitters of the past can human judgment be moderately pure and unsullied. When they are named, a new element of interest comes in, a conjecture of character and often doubt. Good heavens! Could all Englishwomen of the eighteenth century have been so ravishing as the fashionable painters of the

Portrait of an Old Lady, Ming Dynasty. Collection of G. Del Drago.

day present the Linley sisters, Lady Hamilton, or Mrs. Lovat? Could there have been so many handsome men or charming children? But here they are portrayed for us, nor can sharp-witted words make us disbelieve in them.

Perhaps the secret of portraiture has one clue here: the attempt to catch and hold transfixed another human being in the passage of life, which whirls so wildly past us however calm and static we may try to make it seem. This in real life can't be done; as well try to freeze a wave or bid the wind stand still as try to hold another person in a moment of time. We think it can be done instant by instant, but however we deceive ourselves, the flight of time wings past us all. However, we can have the illusion of doing so, and this is the very heart of portraiture and the reason for it.

The wise and sensible Chinese never seem to demand the unattainable. All they seem to try for in portraiture is a suggestion, almost a statement of a general type. With the famous figures of the distant past they draw the lineaments of the character tradition has set for them. Yang Kuei-fei was a moon-faced beauty, Yo Fei was a great and powerful general, Confucius was a statesman, and there they are, and we in the West are disappointed because we want them more particularized.

9. The Palaces of Ch'in

THE processes of living and thinking must have been much simpler at the time when the palaces of Ch'in were burned and the dynasty fell. Ch'in (221–206 B.C.) was a very short dynasty, but it must have been a thoroughly uncomfortable fifty-odd years for those conservative people who had to live through it. (The date when the State of Ch'in took over the empire is 221 B.C. The dynasty really began in 255 B.C.) The first emperor of Ch'in is rather a conspicuous figure in history. We remember him for "the burning of the books" by which he sought to wipe out all the traditions of the past and for the inception of the Great Wall by which he sought to shut the barbarians out. But the books survived and the barbarians came over the wall again and again, so that at long range he does not seem to have broken the course of the evolution of Chinese civilization. It is comforting to think of that, but things were simpler then and the reasons given for the dynasty's fall are simpler too.

There is a worn and faded scroll in the Metropolitan Museum accompanied by a poem. Together, poem and picture present one of those amusing kinds of thinking that occur when conventions which are variable and the element which we call beauty are not quite in agreement. Gibbon despised Catholicism, but his heart betrayed him when he spoke of "the stately monuments of superstition." Poor Ruskin condemned the pagan subjects of the sixteenth century Venetians with similar contradictory phrases which admire while they damn. And we find that what we might with innocent delight suppose to be merely an enchanted fairy palace, with multicolored roofs and infinite variety of court and garden continuing almost endlessly through hills and lakes, peopled by lovely and slender feminine

79

The Palaces of Ch'in (detail), in the tradition of Chao Po-chu (*fl.* 1127–1162). Metropolitan Museum of Art.

figures, is in reality an admonitory illustration of the extravagance which caused the downfall of the Ch'in dynasty.

There are a number of inscriptions accompanying the picture, the first of which purports to be written by Wang Tseng (A.D. 934–1038), a native of T'ai Yuan, who was one of the outstanding statesmen in the Sung dynasty. In 1023 he rose to be president of the Board of Rites, and in 1035 he was appointed lord chamberlain and made a duke. It is a copy of a prose poem by Tu Mu (A.D. 803–852), who was a secretary in the Grand Council of the T'ang dynasty. As a poet he achieved considerable distinction, and is often referred to as the young Tu, to distinguish him from the great poet Tu Fu (712–770). His work on the Ch'in palace was read by every educated Chinese. I give it as paraphrased by Han Shou-hsuan.

"After the six kings had been conquered, the four seas were united into one. After the mountains in Szechwan had become bare, the A-fang Palace appeared. The Palace covered more than three hundred *li* [about a third of a mile] and kept the sky and the sun from being seen. Within the Palace boundaries Mount Li stood in the North and turned to the West, then straightly went into the region of Hsien-yang. There were also two rivers which flowed gently into the walls of the Palace.

"In the Palace there was a tower house within every five feet, one hall within every ten feet, the verandas were continuous and the eaves were tall. Each building occupied suitable ground and each seemed to vie with the other. The buildings were so crowded and so many that they were like the cells of the bee and the waves of the river. So we did not know exactly how many thousands there were.

"The long bridge crossing the river seemed to be a dragon, but how when there was no cloud? Double-roads appeared in the sky like rainbows, but there was no rain. The roads and bridges were so confused that we could not tell East or West.

"The opera hall was warmed by the many singings, so we felt as if the sun were shining in the spring. The dancing hall was cooled by the dancers' sleeves, so we felt as if there were cold wind and rain. Thus within the same day and in the same Palace there were different climates.

"The imperial concubines, princes, and princesses of the six kingdoms had departed from their own palaces and been brought to the Ch'in Palace. They sang in the morning and played music in the evening. So they all became entertainers in the Ch'in Court.

"The bright stars appeared because the imperial concubines used their mirrors while dressing; the dark clouds came because the concubines combed their hair. The Wei River increased because the waste water from the wash bowls of the concubines was poured into the river. The smoke and fog were seen because they burned fragrant incense. The thunder threatened the people because the chariots passed by—the sound could be heard from the far distance, but we did not know where they went. Every imperial concubine was exquisite and voluptuous. They always stood by their doors hoping to see the Emperor's coming—yet some of them might not see the Emperor for thirty-six years.

"The treasures of the Yen and Chao kingdoms, the possessions of the Han and Wei kingdoms, and the treasury of Chi and Ch'u had been carefully selected and stored for generations. They all were obtained from the people and piled up like hills in the six kingdoms. But suddenly the kingdoms could not keep these treasures, so the treasures had to be transferred to the Palace. In the Palace the ceremonial vessels, jade stones, gold, and pearls appeared scattered everywhere; the people in the court never paid any attention to them.

"It was generally accepted that the desire of one man was the same as that of others. As the people of Ch'in liked to have extravagant things, the others also liked to have them. We could not understand why the people of Ch'in had taken everything from the others, then used them carelessly like mud or sand.

"Moreover, the Emperor made the Palace so extravagant that the pillars to support the beams on the roofs were more than the farmers working on the farms, the beams to support the side poles were more than the girls working on the weaving machines, the nails used in the buildings were more than the kernels of grain in the barns, the tiles used on the roofs were more than the silken threads used in clothes, the different railings were more than the cities in the nine regions (that is, the whole nation), the sounds of the flutes and strings were more than the noises made by the people in the markets. Thus did the Emperor make the people angry, but they did not dare to speak any word. He became more haughty and intolerant. Then the garrison rebelled. The strategic pass, Han Ku, fell. The people of Ch'u set fire to the Palace. The Palace became ashes.

"The conqueror of the six kingdoms was the six kingdoms themselves, not the Ch'in kingdom. So also the conqueror of the Ch'in kingdom was Ch'in itself, not the earth under heaven (that is, the Ch'u kingdom). If the six kingdoms had loved their people, they would have been able to resist the Ch'in kingdom. If the Ch'in kingdom had loved the people of the six kingdoms, the Ch'in dynasty would have been able to last from three generations to ten thousand generations and continue to be ruler; certainly there would have been no one to conquer the Ch'in Empire.

"The Ch'in people had no time to pity themselves, but the later generations pitied them. If later generations pity the Ch'in Empire but do not get a lesson from it, they in turn will be pitied by successive generations."

If the painting is meant for a moralistic illustration of this poem, the painter has been led astray—extravagant the palaces may be, but we can see only loveliness and we cannot hear the thunder of the chariots or know that the beams on the roofs were more than the farmers working on the farms. As a sermon I am afraid it fails. As a lovely fantasy (and not so fantastic at that) of the palaces of Ch'in, it is a complete success.

The painting is attributed to Chao Po-chu and is up to the standard of most of the better paintings attributed to him. We have for comparison the paintings mentioned in "Landscapes Green and Blue." Aside from the pleasures of the poem, this particular picture is a fine example of the interest the Chinese painters take in architecture. The Palaces of Ch'in and the Palaces of Han have been painted again and again and again, and so have many other palaces.

A serious student of Chinese architecture can learn much from the stone Han reliefs and the pottery miniatures buried in tombs. He may observe the temples and palaces which appear in successive centuries in the wall paintings of Tun Huang where one whole cave is devoted to a kind of map of the T'ai Shan.

10. Birds, I

*"I am but mad north-north-west: when the wind
is southerly I know a hawk from a handsaw."*

In matters ornithological there are few authorities on Chinese art who can say as much as Hamlet. If they would let well enough alone they would keep out of mischief, because esthetically it does not matter a great deal if a distant bird in flight in a Chinese painting is a white-fronted goose, a bean goose, or even a Jankowski swan (cygnus bewickii jankowski—a millstone of a name for any bird to carry). But they do not let well enough alone. They quarrel, they squabble, they wrangle; sometimes they come very near to brawling.

Not unlike birds are the savants themselves when they congregate for learned conference. In such assemblies the bird-minded cannot but think of crane and owl, of hawk and heron, and of other species lean and hungry, voluble and dignified. Something like this must have been in the minds of the Chinese when they chose birds as appropriate insignia for their civil officials, including in the higher ranks the lordly peacock and the melancholy crane, in the lesser ranks the retiring quail and the loquacious oriole.

The art experts are funny enough, but when they call in the ornithologists the confusion and tumult are greatly increased. At the Princeton conference of 1947 a minor altercation took place between two authorities as they confronted each other before a very good version in the Morris collection of the painting generally known as Hui Tsung's White Eagle. One protested at a suggestion that this great white bird be called a golden eagle. The other, triumphant, quoted a famous ornithologist to the effect that, as there is no such thing as a white eagle, the bird must be an albino golden eagle; whereupon the first retorted that albinos have pink eyes and Hui Tsung's eagle's eyes are yellow. In the end the dispute was resolved by labeling Princeton's bird succinctly "Eagle."

The bitterest strife, of course, is about the birds which appear in the highly conventionalized designs of the early Chinese ceremonial bronzes; particularly those, on a series of early vessels, which have for a long time been called owls and quite recently have been put forward as pheasants—and tragopan pheasants at that. The question is far from settled. It is obvious that in later Chinese art a pheasant is the unmistakable progenitor of the Flowery Bird of the twelve sacrificial symbols and of the feng huang, mistakenly called phoenix; and it is true that the owl appears much less often in Chinese art and literature than the pheasant. It is also obvious that in the formalized and symbolic decoration of bronzes of the Shang dynasty (about 1558 to about 1050 B.C.) representations of a bird are intended. They are, however, so highly conventionalized that it is surprising that anyone in his right senses would try to determine from them even a genus, far less a species. Who but Western scholars of the twentieth century would squabble over the species of these birds of three thousand years ago?

Is not the important thing that in the symbolism of the early Chinese a Beast and a Bird played a great part? Does it matter much which bird, which beast? While our iconographers bicker and wrangle over the bull and ram, the tiger and water buffalo, the pheasant and owl, most of them persist in ignoring the answer to the magnificent rebus of the *t'ao t'ieh*, that interlocking composite of bird and beast which is the symbol of one fundamental precept of Chinese thinking—the balanced dualism of *yin* and *yang*, of darkness and light, of moon and sun, of female and male.

Creel, in *The Birth of China*, demonstrated most of the elements of this rebus. He pointed out—and no one has contradicted him—that, if you bisect the mask of the front-facing monster, you will find that the two halves of the design may be read as profile pictures of beast facing beast nose to nose. He also demonstrated that the same profile may be read backwards, in which case the hindquarters of the beast become a bird facing in the other direction. Only one thing remained: to demonstrate that the bird, full face, with wings outspread, is an integral part of the front-facing mask. This was most ably done in the November, 1938, issue of The Metropolitan Museum of Art *Bulletin*, a publication, light in weight but rich in content, into which many such jewels are cast.

While we are making merry over the contentiousness of picture-critics and ornithologists we are flirting with a very serious difference between two things which should not necessarily be in opposition but often seem to be—the difference between art and science. Is there any good reason why an artist should not paint a bird accurately enough to content a scientist? Would anyone dare to say that a bird inaccurately limned is more pleasing than a bird correctly drawn? Look from Audubon's Golden Eagle to Hui Tsung's White Eagle, from Audubon's Snowy

Egret to the Egret after Chao Tzu-ku in the Metropolitan Museum, from Audubon's Cedar Waxwing to the Chinese Waxwing in the Philadelphia Museum.

But before we arrive at our conclusion, which will be, of course, that Chinese painters have always done everything better than anyone else, let us diverge for a moment to look at birds as depicted in American guidebooks by illustrators selected by the ornithologists themselves. There are a number of notable bird-painters, including Louis Agassiz Fuertes, Francis Lee Jacques, Roger Tory Peterson, Lloyd Sandford, Allan Brooks, and Don Eckelberry, and many more are coming up.

It is interesting to observe that, more and more, in our American bird guides drawings are preferred to photographs (a fact which gives pleasure to those of us who think the camera lies more frequently than it tells the truth). It is interesting to note also that, more and more, the bird-painters show the birds in varied action. Furthermore, and to the advantage of scientific bird-observers, the illustrations for such books as Roger Tory Peterson's bird guide have achieved, by the *elimination* of almost everything but shape outlines and outstanding markings, "a 'boiling down,' or simplification, of things so that any bird could be readily and surely told from all the others at a glance or at a distance." Now what is this? art or science? or, for once, art and science walking happily hand in hand?

Yet even the best of bird pictures cannot exactly represent a bird. I knew one fourteen-year-old bird boy who hurled his Christmas gift of Audubon indignantly at his offended parents (who had sought to please him), because, he said, the pictures therein did not look like the birds. He was quite right. He knew his birds in field and swamp, alive and singing on the wing. Pictures drawn from taxidermists' birds wired on branches disgusted him. Your true birdlover must have his birds alive and preferably wild in their own habitat. For the scientist, however, no picture will do at all; he must have the real bird, alive or dead (although at least one naturalist, with Walrus tears, expressed regret when he felt forced to murder a rare warbler in Central Park to prove that he had seen it there—an operation which made a rare species rarer still).

If we may go so far—that is to say that no picture can exactly represent a bird — it would appear that all paintings of birds should be considered art. (Art, of course, is a word which did not invade the Chinese language until quite recently, but it is so much used in America that it cannot always be conveniently avoided.) As there still seems to be a considerable divergence of opinion as to what is art and what is illustration, where pictorial representation is concerned, for the present discussion may we not say that the instant one leaves the actual bird—the instant one resorts to paper and brush—the result is art, good or bad as the case may be?

All paintings of birds are art. On the basis of this assumption we may forego the

Egret after Chao Tzu-ku (*fl.* 1226–90), Sung style. Metropolitan Museum of Art.

bootless quarrel between art and science and discover that the argument turns into something like a personal prejudice in favor of what, for want of better terminology, we call realism or impressionism.

With this in mind let us look at the bird guides of, say, the past fifty years. The illustrations in the early books in this series are hopefully realistic, but, wonder of wonders, as the century progresses they become simpler and livelier. It would seem either that impressionism has been seeping in or that the illustrators have been consciously trying to fuse realism and impressionism. Actually, it is not that the painters have had any intention of sacrificing correctness but that they have been trying to present birds as our eyes see them at a distance, not dead in the hand, and that in doing so they have been adding suggestions—realistic impressions—of the birds' movements. As a result, in place of the meticulous drawings and colored photographic reproductions of badly stuffed goldfinches and tanagers of the early twentieth century, we now have, as has already been noted, Roger Tory Peterson's simplifications and the lively pages that Don Eckelberry has recently done for Richard Pough's *Audubon Bird Guide*.

Whence came this happy change? The answer could be very simple. It could be that, as we strive to adapt our educational system to the inevitable changes time brings to us with increasing rapidity, the labors of the United States Department of Agriculture and of the Audubon Society are bearing fruit. It could be that, in the campaign for conservation, the attempt to halt the tragic ravages upon our wild-life made by the rapacious nineteenth century, our bird-guide illustrators have been developing, of their own volition, a way of representing birds which will not only inform but charm a greater public. It could be as simple as that.

But when we look back to the early nineteenth century (Audubon) and the eighteenth century in Europe (Nozeman) we find that bird books were both informative and pleasing to look at. The charm of birds is not a modern American discovery. It was known to Western civilization. For a short time it seems to have been lost; but it is being recovered.

Just when did the West discover the charm of birds, particularly of birds by themselves or in compositions of flowers? It is undesirable here to diverge into a history of birds in Western art—to skim from the geese of ancient Egypt or its hawk- and vulture-headed gods, to be diverted by the sensational career of the eagle from Greek myth to national emblem of such different governments as Czarist Russia and the Presidential United States, or to look into the symbolism of the pelican and the dove in the *Four Mirrors* of the medieval encyclopaedist Vincent of Beauvais. Yet it would be interesting to discover at what point Western artists began to paint birds, not merely as accessories or symbols, but by themselves.

Think of the woodeny birds surrounding St. Francis in Giotto's chapel at Assisi, or the stiff fowl in the monastery garden in Carpaccio's St. Jerome Taming the Lion, in Venice. Surely it was not until the eighteenth century that birds began to be pictured as really lively and important for themselves, represented in what are almost stage scenes of flowering trees and ornamental rocks. Was this a European invention? Of course it wasn't. It must have been inspired by the importations of ornamental vases and wallpapers from the Orient. Our histories of art are well aware of the influence of Chinese art upon the decoration of the eighteenth century, but has it occurred to our naturalists that possibly it influenced their way of representing birds and flowers too?

Those gaudy color plates made for Buffon (Georges-Louis Leclerc de Buffon, *Histoire naturelle, générale et particulière avec la description du cabinet du roi*, volumes 16–24, published in Paris, 1770–1783) are like enough, many of them, to Chinese work to have been plucked bird by bird from one of the cruder wallpapers. That enchanting frontispiece for Cornelius Nozeman's *Nederlandsche Vogelen*, with a galaxy of birds swinging on branch and rush, isn't there at least a whiff of China here? There is no evidence that naturalists deliberately copied a way of presenting birds from the Chinese, but may they not have been unconsciously influenced by exposure to Chinese birds and flowers?

Practicing painters are rarely cordial to historians. Why should they be? When one is bent on making pictures of the world as he sees or dreams it, he likes to think it entirely his own creation and usually does not relish being told by outside observers that he is plagiarizing even famous masters of the past. With rare exceptions, he does not even like to have it pointed out that the greater his visual experience of old masters, the richer and profounder is the new thing that he may add to the infinite possibilities of expression. Not for a moment would we have tried to demonstrate to Louis Agassiz Fuertes, for instance, that he might be an American offspring of eighteenth century China. Nevertheless, may we not suspect that in Western painting a new way of looking at birds appeared when the arts and crafts of China became fashionable in eighteenth century Europe?

Once discovered, this new attitude was never entirely lost to the decorative arts. In the bird-book illustrations, however, there seems to have been a break in the tradition, a brief period of doldrums which is now coming to an end. While no one could say that present-day bird-book illustrators are directly influenced by the Chinese (unless some of them come forward to say it themselves), may we not consider the possibility that indirectly the influence is there?

What are the main differences between Western and Chinese painters of birds and flowers? In the painting of birds and flowers, what did Western artists learn from the Chinese?

Snowy Egret by John J. Audubon, original water color for Plate 242 of *Birds of America.* Courtesy of the New-York Historical Society.

There is no question of the interest of Western man in nature from earliest times; one has only to regard, for example, the capitals in medieval churches or the myriad birds and flowers of the Unicorn tapestries at The Cloisters, where many species are most accurately and carefully depicted. It is the Western attitude that is different from the Chinese.

Western artists delineate things in nature with care, but they usually subordinate them as parts of a grand scheme in which human beings are the most important elements. The Chinese, on the other hand, painted birds for their own importance as early as the Sung dynasty (960–1279), treating them almost as we treat portraits. They have had a tendency to regard the humblest bird, flower, or insect with affection and respect and to represent it with the same dignity and importance that the West has reserved for Man—until, of course, Rosa Bonheur came along to make the harmless lioness look like a sleek matron (sweet creatures both) at the Albert Hall but she is an exception. The Chinese never sentimentalize about birds and grasses, but neither do they underrate them. The European painter tends to favor accuracy, on the whole. The Chinese painter is accurate about certain general aspects, yet for specific details he cares nothing at all. It is his interest to give an impression of a bird, an impression of a bird alive, frozen forever in a moment of time but suggesting always time's flow and movement.

It is difficult, as you see, to try to tell Westerners about Chinese painting or thinking without becoming grandiose. The principles are really very simple, but translations of Chinese terms are bound to sound fancy or quaint. Your Western interpreter, struggle as honestly as he may, sounds at best Maeterlinckian. How can you convey to a practical Yankee from Maine that the Chinese are bent on painting the very souls of trees and rocks and birds, that they sacrifice minute detail in their desire to convey the essential character of a particular kind of tree or rock or bird? Westerners see what they see and are stubbornly practical. But, unwilling as they may be to adopt another point of view, eventually they will learn that the Chinese way of looking at things is a subtle virus and catching.

One cannot blame Western naturalists for finding fault with Chinese painting. It must be irritating to our ornithologists to have Hui Tsung turn up with a White Eagle when there is no such thing as a white eagle. One can sympathize. As West and East fuse, one may even hope that Chinese painters, without losing any of their skill in presenting wings and movement, may make their birds a little more recognizable. Until then, most of us are bound to admire the birds they do present —sometimes alone, almost as portraits; sometimes in rhythmic compositions so satisfactory to the eye that few of us care that they are mind birds, half real, half fanciful. Chinese painters cannot but be aware of the elegance and grace of birds wherever they see them—their ecstasy is in their eyes. They are aware of different shapes, of different kinds of flight. They can indeed tell a hawk from a handsaw, whichever way the wind blows. They can also tell the difference between a hawk and a sparrow quite a lot of the time. But once they have observed the generic differences they really don't care much about the regrettable multiplicity of sparrows—or of ducks—as described by our bird books. Cygnus bewickii jankowski, indeed!

11. Birds, II

"Lost in the spaces I shall hear and bless
The splendid voice of London, like a lion
Calling its lover in the wilderness."
—STELLA BENSON, "The Newer Zion"

SHORTLY before dawn on market days the irritated squealing of pigs can be heard from one end of Peking to the other. One can scarcely blame the pigs, as they are transported upside down with their trotters uncomfortably trussed to poles, and nobody has ever thought of gagging them. Heard far off, the sound is not unpleasant; really, if one did not know what it was, one might well mistake it for an army of bagpipers on the march. But even on the days which are not market days the city of Peking is full of delectable noises. At night the musical street calls of a few peddlers, not unlike the occasional calls of birds in a sleeping forest, are always to be heard, and as the wheel of day comes up bit by bit the sounds increase until at sunrise they become the most glorious din in the world.

The Chinese must really love noise passionately, for they add to all the necessary and expected sounds a great many unnecessary but diverting ones. One would expect in the life of a great city the human babel of crowded streets where traffic proceeds at a dog trot, unhampered by lights. One would expect the rumbling of wheels, the beat of hooves, the neighing of horses, the braying of asses, the angry mumble of camels, the vocal warnings of carters and riksha boys, the constant bands which accompany wedding and funeral processions. In these bands are heard the blaring voices of the foreign brasses, the lugubrious, deep-throated groans of the gigantic horns of the Lamas, the mild singsong of the Buddhists, the lightsome tinkling bells of the Taoists (in a country tolerant to religions all varieties may appear in the same procession—and often do). This should be quite enough for the most interested ear, but the Chinese, not content with noises logical and necessary, have gone out of their way to invent others. The street cries which are few at night are myriad by day, the water carts have been built to emit the most extraordinary and tuneful squeaks to warn traffic of their approach, bells hang from every pagoda eave to catch the wind, caged birds are taught to sing songs they were never born to sing as they are carried by laborers to their places of work, and whole flocks of pigeons are turned loose with an endless variety of little whistles attached to their backs so that a flood of sound comes down from the skies.

There are also the sounds of the wild, uncaged birds which nest in large colonies or alone in the arbor vitae trees of temple courtyards and palace gardens in the Imperial City. One might almost mistake the metropolis for a bird sanctuary. Indeed, before it was named Peking it was called Yenching, the Swallow Capital. Magpies black and white (the "lucky bird"), magpies soft blue with a dab of white in their tails (mountain magpies), warblers, finches, hoopoes, crows fly freely from courtyard to courtyard. The crows, in fact, are such a nuisance that the descendants of the onetime Imperial goldfish which are still nurtured in the spacious grounds of the Altar of Earth—now called Central Park with the well-intentioned but surely mistaken idea that "Central Park" is a more democratic name (let none forget the earth out of which all races and civilizations came and to which all will return)—must be covered with wire netting to keep the crows from plucking out their telescopic, exophthalmic eyes, eyes tempting to any crow.

Birds which would seem to be country birds still more than these inhabit the Forbidden City, its lotus-flowered moat, and the myriad pavilioned gardens of the lake palaces of the South, the Middle, and the North seas. Here are a variety of herons and wagtails, and the elegant jacana. The jacana is a lovely bird. Neatly armored in black and white, with a curved scimitar tail, it greatly resembles a small pheasant, and it is called by the Chinese "water pheasant." At dawn, as the earliest white sunlight irradiates the faded red and yellow of the Forbidden City watchtowers, the jacanas may be seen (and heard) stepping daintily from lily pad to lily pad, accompanied in the proper season by absurd, delightful chicks.

In winter, when the summer birds have gone, the hawks become more noticeable. In winter the lakes and palaces, bereft of summer's greens, are even more brilliant and beautiful. This Imperial City with its palaces and lakes has no peer in fact or fancy among the architectural works of man. Seen from the air as the hawks see it, it can be read almost as the score of a symphony is read, theme and countertheme, movement by movement.

The eye-taking colony of white herons that nest in the deep moss green of the ancient arbor vitae grove of the Ancestral Dynastic Temple of the Imperial City may well be singled out for admiration, especially as the grove is set against the rose red walls and yellow roofs of the temple halls. To the lay eye the herons may appear to lead an enviable life, to the lay ear the perpetual cacophony of heron talk sounds reasonable. How lovely, the layman may think, how lovely to live in surroundings noble and restricted among a race all white and shining. Life in this seeming Paradise looks pretty, but ornithologists know that it is in fact a desperate battle for survival, lived, as all wild bird and animal life is lived, with no illusion or sentiment.

Turning from the wild bird to the tame, from the graceful heron to the portly hen, we discover with regret that community life among domesticated birds is, if anything, an even more bitter struggle. Lately the animal psychologists have produced a horrible exposé of the community life of the common domestic hen. Since Schjelderup-Ebbe, who first noticed the pecking order of hens (social precedence among the hens depends on which one can peck hardest), a long series of scientists, including Guhl and Allee in their recent papers, have occupied themselves with study of the social organization, or hierarchy, in *Gallus domesticus*. Who would have thought that hen life was so organized that some would grow fat and sleek and comfortable and others thin and rangy, each taking its exact place in the hen social scale, with the most abused ones becoming what people nowadays call neurotic? Apparently this is so, and awful parallels might be made to human society. Chickens may be born equal, but they seem to make great haste to establish an unequal social scale with innocent brutality. At the thought that there are hens—red hens, for example—that turn out to be conquering peckers, perhaps we should really be frightened.

What would Karl Marx have made of hens? And what of hens in Russia?

Russia has hens, I know, for I once supped in a lodginghouse in Siberia where they were sharing the kitchen, the chairs, and the bed with their owners. At the time my mind was not concerned with hen society; but, come to think of it, the Soviet hen as observed on that occasion was a very different fowl from the Turkestan hen and the Chinese hen I had lately visited. Is it possible that an archaeologist or anthropologist might reconstruct the varying civilizations of the world if he confined himself to a study of the hen?

Let us pause for a moment and examine the hens of different countries and their representation in art. (Even as we begin we can clearly see that the Chinese hen will come out in actuality and in painted counterfeit as the best of them all, just as everything else seems to do in the long run in China.)

Observe first the American hen; observe it on the farm, at county fairs and metropolitan poultry shows. Except at the latter, what do we see most often? The Rhode Island Red, the Leghorn, and the Plymouth Rock (Bantams, Houdans, Buff Orpingtons, and gamecocks are surely frills in American life). In general, do not these fowl somewhat reflect the people who raise them? They are well cared for in most places and seem to lead useful lives. A few are bred for county fairs,

A Magpie on a Flowering Branch

(Detail). Style of the Sung dynasty (960–1280). Painting on
paper. Metropolitan Museum of Art.

but most American hens stay quietly at home (the motorcar has removed the wayward feminist hen from most roads). The American hen appears very little in art—sometimes as a detail in a farmyard scene, occasionally in advertisement (the most notable instance is the crowing cock of Pathé News), and once in a while the feathers appear in women's hats either in their original state or cleverly dyed to look like something else. The hen in America is, like most of us, a very democratic bird.

The English hen, it would seem, stays in that state of life to which it has been called. Oh, admirable English hen!

What of hens on the Continent? In pictures, at least, there are not many. Among the few there are, however, those by the Dutch painter Melchior de Hondecoeter, who made barnyard fowl a major subject, are outstanding.

French hens? In all the wonderful tapestries, full of birds and animals, that were exhibited at the Metropolitan Museum in 1948 was there a single hen, unless we count domesticated pheasants as hens? The cock, long a symbol of the Republic, appeared in the later tapestries. Save in this role domestic fowl have not often turned up in the pictorial art of France. One brilliant appearance in literature, however, the cock, complete with harem of hens, has made as the magnificent hero of Rostand's *Chantecler*:

> "Toi qui séches les pleurs des moindres graminées,
>   Qui fais d'une fleur morte un vivant papillon,
> Lorsqu'on voit, s'effeuillant comme des destinées,
>   Trembler au vent des Pyrénées
>   Les amandiers du Roussillon."

In Imperial Russia there was the Coq d'Or, of course, but he was more puppet than bird—the sorcerer's stage property, made of papier-mâché and gilt paint. He is not to be admitted into the hen world.

The tail feathers of Italian cocks adorn the hats of the *Bersagliere*; the *Bersagliere* in turn adorn the hats—in the combined militant display it is a question which adorns the other more.

In Germany the goose seems to be preferred to the hen (even the army in its parade step imitates the goose), but neither has a notable place in painting.

The hen in ancient Egypt was a rarity. In a country where animals and combination men and animals appeared among the gods, where we must deal with cats and hippopotami and hawks, the hen was almost left out. Howard Carter has written an article about the domestic fowl, demonstrating that it probably originated from the little jungle fowl, but certainly old Egypt paid scant attention to the species.

Nor did the Greeks. To be sure, cocks were associated with Athena, Socrates

condemned asked that a cock be sacrificed to Asklepios, and in that fanciful hinter-
land of fauns and satyrs, of nymphs and centaurs, there existed creatures half fowl,
half animal—for instance, the hippalektryon, half cock, half horse. Fighting cocks
looking, although Greek, a good bit like the jungle fowls, occur on vases. But, on
the whole, hens appear very little in Greek legend or Greek art.

The jungle fowl itself is a very pretty little bird; in New York it may usually
be seen both at the Natural History Museum and at the Bronx Zoo. Thoreau reminds us of its relation to our own domestic fowl, which he would have liked to
turn loose in the Concord woods. "To walk in a winter morning in a wood where
these birds abounded, their native woods, and hear the wild cockerels crow on the
trees, clear and shrill for miles over the resounding earth, drowning the feebler
notes of other birds—think of it! It would put nations on the alert." (Thoreau was
quite often a trial to his neighbors.)

Leave the West for the East, then what do we find? We find our common barnyard fowl living, in legend and picture at least, a very different life. It has had a
long and important history. Somewhere out of India we think the cock (a stage
version of a Rhode Island Red) came three-legged, to become in China the symbol
of the sun and to rest on the Emperor's shoulder as one of the twelve sacrificial
symbols. This symbol is recorded in the Book of Rites, which was compiled as
early as the fifth century B.C. To this day a white cock rides on coffins in rural
China. He is a symbol, when he appears there, of life and vitality and promise.

Cocks, hens, and chickens are a common—almost a favorite—subject with
painters in both China and Japan. In China cocks and hens are a more conspicuous
feature of the landscape than they are elsewhere—in New England, for instance,
they keep their place as barnyard fowl; they are a small detail in any vista with a
white farmhouse and a red barn. In China there are no white houses or red barns.
There the countless towns and villages are each a sensible huddle of houses—
sometimes built entirely of the lion-colored soil, sometimes with walls of gray
brick—against a tawny ground. In such a setting the cocks and hens are as brilliant
as a Bakst ballet. From one end of China to the other these common fowl shine out.
Most of them are of the variety we call Rhode Island Red—an odd name to give
to poultry that decorate towns and provinces with names that sound like enchant-
ments from the *Arabian Nights*. Very often the plumage of the cocks is of a magnificence and brilliance seeming far to surpass that of New England fowl, and their
manner is surely more lordly. Small wonder that in China they attract the painter's
eye.

One thing about the Chinese that Westerners are instantly sympathetic with but
smile at indulgently, because most Westerners do not think about birds and
animals and flowers as the Chinese do, is the way the Chinese feel about nature.

Hen, Cock, and Chickens (detail), attributed to Huang Ch'uan of Ch'ung Tu (*ca. 919–965*). Ex coll. Bahr, Metropolitan Museum of Art.

East or West, man is fully aware that he is one up on all other forms of life. He is right both East and West. But in their attitude towards nature there is a difference between East and West: Your Westerner knows that he is lord of the universe and rather tiresomely emphasizes it; the Chinese in all their ways are equally secure, but they have an appreciation and respect for the whole natural world that we Westerners do not.

East and West, all men observe the wild goose winging and smile at the amusing antics of mice. But the Chinese, when they stop to think of nature, think something that most Westerners do not. They see, almost without thinking, what our Darwins and others try to tell us: that, while we are certainly more complicated than a mouse or hen, in our life cycle—in the natural order of things—the mouse and I, the mouse and you, the hen and I, the hen and you, have much in common experience. Man, being first of all an animal, must perforce pass through a physical life scheme similar to that of other animals (and never should man forget this); yet aeons and aeons ago the human animal began to create a world of mind and spirit, which is the one you and I live in and which we strive to perfect. All men know this, though they seem to forget it and snarl up their heritage. Both West and East will learn—indeed, have learned—to express the likeness in the life experience of animals and human beings, but they say and picture it in different ways.

Your Westerner is likely to be kinder to animals than your Easterner, but he is also likely to attribute to animals and birds the complicated emotional scheme in

97

Hen, Cock, and Chickens (detail), attributed to Huang Ch'uan of Ch'ung Tu (*ca.* 919 965). Ex coll. Bahr, Metropolitan Museum of Art.

which human beings themselves live. This comes out best in Kenneth Grahame's *The Wind in the Willows* and Beatrix Potter's mice and rabbits.

Now, the Chinese view the world about them quite differently. They observe and paint mice and men and mountains—and birds—with almost equal dignity and understanding. In legend and fairy lore, however, they seem to view animals much as Westerners do. In China the snake and fox appear in the guise of beautiful women to make appropriate mischief. The dragon has nine misogynous sons, who appear in architectural decoration. The monkey who was a deity in India continues in China to be at least an Immortal. In such matters East and West have likenesses. But apart from this—discarding this phase—remember that, fundamentally, the East thinks, sees, feels differently from the West about animals and birds. Westerners consider themselves either conquerors or victims of the natural world; the Chinese feel themselves a part of it.

Out of India came the idea of the transmigration of souls, the never-ending struggle of the human soul to attain perfection. To Westerners, when they play with this idea at all, it is an amusement that a human being might well live again as a weasel or an egret according to his just deserts; the monkey lover of the *Spectator* papers, the vindictive otter of the Saki stories, are examples. The idea of transmigration was at one time deeply believed in the East. In our day it is probably not deeply believed as a threat, and most Buddhists I think feel that they themselves are safe from such a punishment; but they believe in the possibility; certainly they feel themselves to be part of the animal world.

Thus in the East, out of these roots, comes an attitude towards nature different from the Western attitude, and it shows in all its pictorial record. One does not have to understand the Eastern attitude to take pleasure in a Chinese landscape or flower painting or portrait of a hen, for the eye itself is satisfied; but the mind behind the eye is surely that much richer if it does.

Hens and their ways, when we discover how horribly like they are to human ways superficially, make us laugh, whereas your Chinese philosopher and painter only smiles at them. He is never sentimental about the hen, but he places it and paints it as a dignified and proper creature in the world he lives in. The Chinese are fully aware of the place of the human being in the scheme of nature, but they can understand and see that all life is part of the same scheme—and paint what they see. Man knows in China where he stands in time. He bends and smiles as he watches the life cycle of the hen or the flower; he bows in awe at his relation to the majesty of mountains and the power of the sea.

12. Birds, III

"Seek'st thou the plashy brink
Of weedy lake, or marge of river wide,
Or where the rocking billows rise and sink
On the chafed ocean-side?

"There is a Power whose care
Teaches thy way along that pathless coast—
The desert and illimitable air—
Lone wandering, but not lost."

—WILLIAM CULLEN BRYANT
"To a Waterfowl"

Two women sat seeming listless on the observation platform of a train lumbering west across the Canadian plains. One presented the appearance of the ideal grand dame, as indeed she was, complete with a tower of closely packed white curls and a hat which was an edifice. One could not swear to white kid gloves, but I think there were. The other was aggressively tweedy and booty with her magnificent braid of dark hair concealed under a hat which looked like a finch's nest turned upside down. Both had joined a small party of tourists going to China and Japan. They had met the night before at Moose Jaw. At this point of their acquaintance they were taking measure of each other, on paw toe so to speak, in the manner in which elegant dogs make overtures to each other in the park. They had said good morning, but after that conversation was so desultory that it hardly could be called conversation at all until three crows flapped heavily across the receding track. At this the second woman lighted up and for a moment forgot humans in her lively interest at the sight of wings. "Oh," she happily exclaimed, "three crows together —that is good luck." The dowager instantly crushed her. "I am afraid," she said, "that you are not very well informed about auguries. If you noticed these birds did not fly from right to left, they flew from left to right, and that is a very bad omen indeed."

It was in fact a simple declaration of war. While we sneer at diplomacy as practiced by our State Department one can sympathize with the cautious delicacy with which it must treat the simplest negotiation—a broken fan, a tiny snub can get nations into war.

The birds are always with us. The sad nightingale of Keats and the radiant skylark of Shelley sing in the heart and are part of the mind fabric of any English-speaking child—lovely creatures both. But birds can be mischievous too, like these crows, or the unwelcome prothonotary warbler that turned up in that most unhappy controversy between Mr. Whittaker Chambers and Mr. Alger Hiss. And the cackling geese that saved Rome must have irritated the invading hordes a good bit.

The birds can be studied and catalogued—beyond that why should they be explained? My favorite author on this subject is the Viscount Grey of Fallodon, K.G. He likes the bird and all wild life. "It is," says he, "just because this wild life is amoral, not troubled by question of right and wrong, that we find it so refreshing and restful." You may twist that statement anyway you like, but the more you ponder upon it the more addled you will get.

The truth of the matter is that the Western mind is always cataloguing and explaining, and, doing it brilliantly well, forgets all sorts of obvious things. There is no doubt that as far as brains, imagination, and the ability to record and transmit experience man has a power which he believes that the animal, the insect (bees and ants sometimes startle him), and the plant world have not achieved. All civilized human beings seem to be agreed on that point.

As to the birds—why has it never occurred to us that we watch them with envy and delight because they have achieved, unmechanized and wordless, the power of flight and of song which the Western mind so desperately strives for. Often and often the Western mind succeeds—it takes wing and sings. Nobody yet knows just how, but it has left traces these four thousand years. In this thing human beings might notice with comfort that when it comes to birds the lower orders of animals are quite as puzzled and distrustful in their way as we are. It is true of most animals. They can not fly and they do not quite like anything as sizable as even a small bird flying. The common cat does not like it at all and has spent incalculable centuries trying to put birds out of existence. Dogs usually give up chasing them early. There are exceptions, but in general the animal world, two-footed or four-, is not quite easy about the birds. We cannot fly and they can. We admire, we envy, but we do not quite like it. (Flying machines are no solution—the greatest man-made machine may suddenly crumple of itself where no bird's wing ever fails. Birds may be beaten down by the wind and forced to earth, but never just crackle and break.)

101

Chinese Bulbuls, by an unknown painter, probably of the Sung Dynasty (960–1280). Ex coll. Bahr, Metropolitan Museum of Art.

China is a vast country. Its flora and fauna are all but countless and their variety is unending. But they have never catalogued them the way Westerners have, so that our orderly knowledge is far from complete. Westerners like order and like names—common names and Latin names for birds and flowers, and it is a never-ending trouble to us that while the Chinese have painted birds and flowers for centuries they are rarely what we call accurate about it. Many species are recognizable, many are almost recognizable—one cannot mistake the egret, the Mandarin duck nor the Manchurian crane, for instance—but the professional or determined amateur botanist or ornithologist has a very hard time indeed. The Chinese in their pictures do not go in for realism in the sense that Westerners do. Their picture world is derived, of course, from the real world—it is a fantasy world but not a deliberate fantasy. Birds and flowers are pretty things, and birds and flowers they paint not for accuracy but for pleasant pictures to look at. Westerners finding a scroll entitled The Hundred Birds or The Hundred Flowers think momentarily they have run into the beginnings of a flower or bird book. They have not. The Chinese like the sound of "The Hundred Flowers" and "The Hundred Birds" and forthwith paint a medley of flowers or birds. Admirers of Chinese painting try to explain to us, and it is a very hard thing to explain, that in everything they do the Chinese are painting not the exact exterior of flowers and birds but the living spirit—the inner reality of the flower or bird in visual terms. So they are, but it is hard for most of us to see.

Certain things we can see, and see quickly. The Chinese paint birds and flowers much more universally than any school of European or American painting. It is hard to imagine a Chinese house without some picture of flowers or birds, whereas in an American house birds and flowers are mostly relegated to prints—flower prints in the bedroom or stairs, game birds perhaps in the den.

If I make too much of the birds it is because I like them myself East and West, and the difference between the way East and West approach them is a clue to the whole pattern of Chinese life, or at least to the whole way the Chinese look at life in their picture world.

The Chinese way of looking at things is often maddening to the amateur Western botanist or ornithologist. It is the more maddening because while you cannot be sure of the exact species of flowers or bird you are looking at ninety-nine times out of a hundred, they suggest real flowers and real birds more than do even the birds and flowers of Western scientific books.

Even in the business of egrets and cranes—handy decorative birds for any painters—except for an Audubon record or the joke about the crane delivering babies, where do these birds appear in Western art? Rarely, but they and countless others appear constantly in Oriental everyday painting simply for pure visual pleasure.

Easy to say, and probably part of the secret is caught in a transitory movement.

Long ago after Westerners, amused with the lively antics of Oriental horses in painting, took moving pictures of a horse in action they were startled to find that centuries ago the East approximated it. So with birds, so with flowers—so with rain and moving streams, so with the wind, so with flames. We can understand technical tricks—line can suggest movement and by line all these things are made to move. If that is the trick, Westerners have used it very little. Those magnificent blurs of Turner's—Rain, Wind and Speed—the Nocturnes of Whistler (himself aware of the Orient), come to mind. These Orientals paint not only what you see—they paint the forces behind what you see. The Chinese are painters of the wind and rain—the bent bamboo, the billowing line of a tiny sail informs us of the presence of the wind. They paint storms and seasons and times of day—they paint heat and cold. Almost any lotus flower conveys the tranquil hotness of July, the Hsia Kuei in the Boston Museum of Art has the sense of a severe shower about to break.

Perhaps man unconsciously feels more proud in winter—leaves fall, flowers fade, most birds fly south from it, most animals hibernate; but man puts on an extra coat and builds a fire—he and a few shy wild things face a world stripped of summer's warmth and comfort. He alone can see and feel the majesty of bare hills and the stark skeleton beauty of trees denuded of their leaves. Only the

Marsh Scene with Birds (detail), attributed to Shen Chou (1427–1509). Ex coll. Bahr, Metropolitan Museum of Art.

Chinese and, after them, the Japanese have learned to present winter in all its beauty. Courbet's winter is damp and snowy enough; Turner's snowstorms, once you are told what they are, can be appreciated as virtuoso tricks; and certainly the early Dutch and, before them, the illuminated manuscripts paint winter scenes and paint them well; but there is more emphasis on bewoolened human beings than there is on winter. Only the Easterners present winter as winter itself—as a season, as a major force of nature, cold and powerful and splendid.

In 1951 the Fogg Museum of Art of Harvard University presented an exhibition called Masterpieces of Chinese Bird and Flower Painting. This included thirty-five paintings from American collections accompanied by an excellent catalogue and introductory essay by Benjamin Rowland.

Birds appear in the Shang bronzes of three thousand years ago where they play a symbolic role and are represented in intricate and highly formalized design.

By the time we reach the Han dynasty (206 B.C.–A.D. 220) a good many kinds of birds are recognizable. Sometimes they play a symbolic role, sometimes they are merely being hunted, as on Han pottery jars.

In the T'ang dynasty (618–906) they are an accepted part of decoration; pheasants and ducks, geese and little birds abound on the little silver boxes and mirrors of the period. One pheasant, glorified as the feng huang ("the Oriental phoenix") appears on the tiaras of Imperial women both in painting and actual relics.

By the tenth century birds and flowers, alone or together, had become a favorite subject for formal painting. Single birds in hanging paintings or in album leaves came into the scene and came to stay. The emperor Hui Tsung painted a White Eagle that has been copied so often through the centuries that it would seem that almost every self-respecting collector East or West must have one. A parakeet on an album leaf is almost as common. One attributed to him and much admired is in the Boston museum. There is little doubt that as well as these single birds and birds in pairs, birds in flocks or in mixed congregation were painted in the Sung dynasty, but we quite rightly believe that the sets of twelve paneled screen paintings and single hanging painting of lush and gorgeous design were a Ming development and continued down to the present day.

The birds are very much with us in Chinese painting. Beautiful examples of bird and flower painting are owned by most American museums, and countless thousands decorate American homes.

Whether you prefer a bird singly or a hundred birds amid flowering trees and plants is a good deal a matter of personal taste. I myself am no very good adviser in this matter because I like birds whether they are alive and out of doors or painted and indoors—I like them real or fanciful. The ones familiar to me in both worlds give me greater pleasure when I see them in painting. The most casual traveler in the Far East cannot but be aware of them. Even in the great city of Peking the white egrets, the hawks, the magpies, and the wagtails of the paintings are familiar things. Journey through the countryside and he must see as in the paintings flocks of Manchurian cranes in stately dance and equally stately flight. At dusk in the villages white-collared crows noisily come to roost, over the Hami oasis in Turkestan the sound of larks pours down like rain, swallows nesting in the inns awaken you at dawn as they dart in and out on light gymnastic wing. Surely it must please to see them caught however fleetingly in a picture large or small.

13. Tribute Horse

A SMALL but brilliantly caparisoned cavalcade proceeding from the northwest towards the Sung Court of Pien Ching came suddenly to an opening in the rocky pass which gave on a view of broad plain with a great cathedral mass of mountain in the middle distance and faint snow-clad peaks beyond.

The cortege was a princely one and well worth looking at. The central figure curiously enough was not a human being but an exceptionally fine white horse in complete harness but without a rider. The bridle was ornamented with cunningly wrought bits of gilt bronze, and a large and handsome red tassel depended from its throat. The animal was saddled, but the saddle was concealed by a covering of pale green damask on which had been worked in gold thread a design of five-clawed dragons. A groom on a handsome bay led the white horse by a halter, and ahead of them rode two outriders carrying banners of state.

Immediately behind ambled two mounted Tatar warriors, swarthy of aspect and accoutered, horse and men alike, in unparalleled magnificence. Over their boots and trousers they wore large loose panels (neither greaves nor chaps but garments designed for somewhat the same purpose) which glittered like dragon scales and which were bordered with the tiger-claw pattern that has long been a prerogative of military dress in China. Their corselets, indeed the whole upper part of their persons, were covered by loose jackets of soft pink silk. The helmets were apparently of gold-plated metal elaborately cast with curling feathers, almost wings at the sides, the same kind of helmet which is to be seen on many of the guardian kings of the east and west, of the north and south, as they were painted on the simulated vaults of the Buddhist cave temples of Tun Huang in the ninth and tenth centuries. Each warrior carried a staff from which fluttered long pennons of white

The Tribute Horse, Sung Dynasty (960–1280). Metropolitan Museum of Art.

and red and black. The trappings of the horses were no less splendid than the regalia of their masters. They wore light neck and tail coverings of red silk sparkling with tiny embroidered gold medallions and fantastic masks of plated gold fashioned like the riders' helmets with flaring feathers—such masks as have only one parallel, which is in a banner painting from Tun Huang. On their rumps they wore round green silken cushions weighted with curious ornaments of bronze and gilt akin to those which are often seen on pottery horses from T'ang tombs.

These gorgeous soldiers kept close to their charge, the white horse, but they could and did ride at ease surveying with pride the progress of that animal and looking from time to time over their shoulders at the rest of the party. This consisted of two grooms bearing ceremonial maces like that depicted in the tenth century wall paintings of Wan Fo Hsia and like the actual mace in the collection of the Metropolitan Museum of Art; a red-robed official and attendant bowman. The whole group of horsemen numbered only ten and they rode at an easy trot

The Tribute Horse (detail), Sung Dynasty (960–1280). Metropolitan Museum of Art.

of the Hua Shan itself. Behind it, right and left in the remote distance, were the mere ghosts of snowy peaks as we see them in paintings attributed to the famous Sung painter Kuo Hsi. Few growing things were to be seen, spare grasses in the foreground, the gnarled pine at the left, a single burst of autumn red on the heights, two or three nearly dead sentinel pines on the rocks at the right and in the foreground an ancient pine twisted but still magnificent.

One man saw this transient worldly cortege as it crossed the great bleak landscape and, being not only profoundly thoughtful but also a very great painter, he had the power to catch and set down on silk the essence of what he saw. This he did, and now after nearly a thousand years something of what he thought and what he saw has come down to us.

The name of the painter is not known, but he must have lived in the early Sung

Dynasty (960–1280). Many details of landscape are close to those which appear in later paintings attributed to Kuo Hsi (*circa* 1020–1090), but this may well be an earlier painting than his.

The towering pine tree in the right foreground is to be found in a fine landscape illustrated in Plate 73 of *The Pageant of Chinese Painting*; the convoluted branches of the tree at the extreme left, through which we catch glimpses of banners, are to be found in another, reproduced in Plate 69 of the same book; and the distant landscapes placed right and left of the great central cliff and the mountaintop itself, as well as the middle river landscape, have likenesses to a painting in the Bahr collection attributed to Kuo Hsi. But without pressing the resemblance to this particular artist, it can be shown that every element of the landscape has its analogy in paintings that today we are sure belong to the early Sung period. The great retreating cliffs at the left are close to those in the large landscape in Boston attributed to Fan Kuan, and the incredible gully in the left foreground has the authority of the landscape details of Boston's Hokkei *mandala*. The red trees at the left are like those in The Deer Park, a painting from the Chinese Imperial Collection that was shown in London in the winter of 1935–1936 to the awe of all who saw it. Inch by inch and detail by detail our picture can be linked to the best we know of early Chinese landscapes.

But there is something else in this picture—the mundane procession that moves boldly across the landscape and dares to assume an equal importance. Now, this is a rare thing and one to pause over. The Chinese love to paint majestic landscapes with tiny philosophers sitting tranquilly in them or tiny processions threading their gorgeous way in and around great hills. We are told that this is because the Chinese realize man's place in time and space, that he is a tiny creature compared with the hills and the sun and moon. But we are also told, and rightly again, that though his span seems short (as against that of a mountain or even a pine tree) man may have a spaciousness of mind that is timeless, so that when we see a tiny philosopher under a great pine tree looking calmly at distant mountain ranges we can judge his quality by the height of the pine and the grandeur of the peaks. Although this is one of those aftertruths got up to explain an impression, some such intuitive idea may have unconsciously commanded these paintings.

The peculiar thing about our picture is that across one of the most majestic of Chinese landscapes there moves a procession of riders, bepomped and glittering, so sure of themselves that they seem completely unaware of the scene through which they pass. If this were a European painting we could say, "Here is the Renaissance—man taking over his birthright." In late Chinese painting, it is true, there are pictures in which man dominates the landscape, rarely in early Chinese painting; and not either in early or in late Chinese painting have I seen one in

The Tribute Horse (detail), Sung Dynasty (960–1280). Metropolitan Museum of Art.

which the interest is equally balanced. In this respect our picture seems to be what biologists call a sport. One might, however, advance an explanation for it: as a courtly compliment the painter was depicting the passage of one of the famous tribute horses of the T'ang emperor T'ai Tsung. (If so, this is the only time a painter weighed Imperial glory against immortal hills.) Such a suggestion may go too far in guesswork, but something of the sort is happening.

The procession itself, without the landscape, is an enchanting thing and full of clues to help us place the picture. Its accouterments have analogies to those in T'ang paintings (these are the gewgaws), but its essential elements are those of early Sung. We may therefore guess at a T'ang subject painted by a Sung artist. Among the details that by themselves can be compared to T'ang counterparts we have the trappings of the horses, the huge tassels depending from the bridles, the bits of bronze on the reins, the masks of the horses (which are elsewhere to be found only in a sketch from Tun Huang), the gilt-bronze-trimmed caparisons on the rumps of the horses of the Tatar warriors, the helmets of the warriors themselves, the emblems of office on the outriders (as in the frescoes of Wan Fo Hsia) —no end of details have their analogies with those of T'ang pictures. The horses themselves and the easy postures of their riders, however, are Sung. (Remember the stiff-legged T'ang horses in pottery and on the walls of Tun Huang, and then the low-slung, furry beasts of Sung as they are in the four panels of The Return of the Lady Wen Chi in Boston and in the album leaf in the Metropolitan Museum.) The riders, too, are depicted with a certain pleasantness and lack of austerity that is characteristic of Sung painting. Surely these are Sung horses and Sung riders.

There are several technical features in the painting for which we cannot as yet find any parallels. Two main schools of landscape painting developed in the T'ang period—one the highly colored school of Li Ssu-hsun, a dazzlement of green and blue cliffs often touched on the outlines with gold; the other, the monochrome school of Wang Wei, associated with the contemplative Ch'an sect of Buddhism— mystic and poetical. This landscape rightfully belongs to the second class, but it is a contradiction because the great receding shoulder of a cliff at the left is edged with soft smudges of gold that bring the light upon it with wondrous luminosity. This is the main part of the landscape so treated, and it is to be noticed that it is the cliff behind the imperial tribute horse. Furthermore, the rocks in the foreground have three subtle shades of color. Scarcely more than a suggestion, but quite definitely there in pale, neutral shades, are a faint blue, terra cotta, and yellow. This is something that we have not seen before.

The picture is without documentary evidence (save in its inherent qualities). It has no signature, real or false, and the remains of two collectors' seals are illegible. It was purchased in Peking from a lesser dealer a few years back by a collector of great judgment and discernment, and was brought to New York and acquired by Charlemagne E. Wells, from whom the Metropolitan Museum bought it. With the enormous mass of material in the Orient it is not surprising that such things occasionally happen, particularly when a country is as troubled as China has been. Sometimes after the event we can trace back a history and an ownership; it is to be hoped that we can do so with this.

By some miracle the painting, which, if one looks close, is badly damaged, has scarcely—if indeed at all—been retouched. There was an instant's doubt about the faces of the Tatar horseman to the left and the halberdier immediately following the warriors, but the closest inspection with a magnifying glass shows no trace of overpainting, and it seems to have been a deliberate and successful attempt of the artist to characterize the coarseness of the Tatar and the groom.

This is a very great picture that is certain to give endless pleasure to those who see it. Splendid as it is as a whole, in detail it is almost inexhaustible. At first glance one sees the austere splendor of the landscape and the great pine trees; one sees the glittering procession and feels the movement of the almost musical pattern of the horses' hooves and the light breeze animating the pennons. With leisure one is aware of the fine rocks in the foreground and follows back to the distant landscapes right and left of the central range of mountains. In the middle foreground there is a river landscape, and each tree is a beauty in itself. There seems to be in this whole picture no corner, no brush stroke even, that is without purpose and meaning.

14. Tun Huang

FAR in the west of China, near the border of Chinese Turkestan, lies the small oasis of Tun Huang. Ten miles across a desert of wind-sculptured dunes which blaze tawny gold and violet in sun and shadow are the Ch'ien Fo Tung, the Cave Temples of the Thousand Buddhas. These are cut into the tightly packed sand and gravel cliff, some hundred and fifty feet high, which was chiseled out by the annual flood season of an ancient river. In May the river is reduced to a tiny trickle with a fringe of fluttering aspen trees.

The traveler of today comes upon the Grottos of the Thousand Buddhas up a valley just as the famous Chinese traveler Hsuan Tsang came upon them in the seventh century. There is a difference in desert places, but all that I have ever seen share certain things in common: light and air and space. A few days west of Tun Huang there is a terrifying march described by Hsuan Tsung, and now as then littered with the bones of pack animals who have died along the way. Hsuan Tsung, of course, saw devils and apparitions—we with an up-to-date, brand-new education know that these are but mirages but get a little frightened in a world where a range of mountains looking perfectly solid floats into the air and melts like a water ice, and where bands of horsemen in a cloud of dust converge upon the highroad. Oh, yes, says the twentieth century traveler, the light does something to a clump of desert grass as we jog by.

Hsuan Tsung described the rising devil chorus at nightfall. It is still there—at nightfall as the sands cool there is first a silence and then a breath of sound, an infinitesimal decrepitation which grows into a desert wind which cracks and breaks into snatches of sound like cries of human anguish. Educated and wise you may be, and so able to account for it in classroom terms. You are educated, Hsuan Tsung was not; but, some thirteen hundred years apart, you have the same senses and the same nervous system, and for all your wisdom you will feel the same dread and awe our ancestors felt some fifty million years ago. Western scientists, geologists, and astronomers toss vast distances and millions of years about like tennis balls, and the modern educated man never turns a hair. This he accepts because it is science, and smiles blithely at the naïveté of the Hindu and Buddhist holy books because, if you please, they are extravagant when they describe kalpas (tens and tens of thousands of years) and talk about thrones a mile high. This is a fine silliness. It comes to the same thing. Western man since the Renaissance must start small and build from facts, he must prove things in physical terms. But in no time at all he is tossing about millions of light years, and building enormous mirrors to prove (what he has known all along) that he cannot quite yet set up a customs station at the frontier of infinity. The East goes at it in exact reverse. They have long been aware of the immensity of the universe, but instead of starting with man and facts and building up a factual universe they have been trying by means of human perception to bring these same ideas down into the range of the human spirit and imagination. It will come to the same thing at long last—no doubt of it, but it may take a few more fretful centuries to arrive.

At Tun Huang there are hundreds of cave temples large and small. One at least is a hundred feet high, some are scarcely more than three feet deep. The late Paul Pelliot counts over two hundred of the more important ones, with subsidiary chapels. The Japanese counting these and small shrines separately numbered many times these. They are tightly packed together like the homes of the cliff dwellers. This series of temples was certainly begun as early as the fifth century and quite probably earlier and is still in use at the present day. There was in 1925 a brand-new one as far as the decoration was concerned. Certainly the temples were still being lavishly decorated as recently as the eighteenth century and still going strong, as innocent visiting archaeologists discovered in the mid-twenties.

Irrespective of size the general plan of all these temples is the same. A square antechamber is cut into the cliff, and a short corridor leads into a much larger inner chamber which is the main hall of the temple. Every inch of the surface of these three rooms except the floor is painted on a coat of plaster so thin that the effect is of true fresco.

In the earlier temples a four-sided "core pillar" has an altar niche cut out of each face of it. Later, as the architects grew more daring, they dispensed with the core pillar and made one large altar at the back wall. In both cases the sculptured gods appear fashioned out of the same earth as the cliff, mixed with plant fibers and baked in the sun. The figures are modeled on a frame of wood. After they have dried out they are coated with thin plaster and painted in the same colors that the walls are painted.

Painting from the South Wall of **Cave** 139A, Tun Huang. Fogg Museum of Art, Harvard University.

116

At one time each temple had a wooden veranda roofed with tiles outside the cliff. Each of these was approached by a wooden staircase entered under a tiled p'ai lou. (A p'ai lou is a kind of horizontal triumphal gate.) The two or three which survived in 1925 were weathered and gray, but they were certainly at one time painted with red lacquer, and it is likely that the tiles shimmered with green or yellow according to princely or Imperial patronage. At one time this place must have outdone Marco Polo and the *Arabian Nights.*

Today it is a magnificent and awesome ruin, if one dare use the word "ruin" for such splendor. White Russians bivouacked there at the time which we call World War I, built fires to keep warm, and so blackened some of the corners. In boredom they scratched dirty words across the faces of the gods. "Dirty words" is merely supposition. They look like dirty words even in a strange alphabet—poor uncomfortable, unhappy creatures to be mewed up in such a place. A prison paradise for an archaeologist—a prison hell for a Russian soldier. Why did not the gentle Buddhist gods smile down and speak to one of them? There are times when one would like to give the ears of the gods a good box.

The damage done by the Russians, while it is conspicuous, amounts to very little in that vast series of caves. Most of it has been done by the forces of nature, by time, and wind and rain. It is a frail cliff, not the "shale" that Stein describes, but merely hard-packed sand, and it has fallen down in great hunks century after century. If one thinks of it in its glory complete with porticos and staircases and so dares use the word "ruin" for it, the word "ruin" is still wrong. It is still magnificent, radiant, and will be while one wall of painted plaster survives.

These wall paintings are mostly as fresh as they were painted, surely from the sixth century down. We have a dated cave there, 538 and 539, Pelliot's cave 120n. This cave has not been repainted and not been retouched. Some of the caves have been recoated and repainted several layers deep, but the top one is always fresh.

So much for a swallow glimpse of the physical appearance of these temples.

In 1925 to reach Tun Huang meant three months of travel, twenty to thirty miles a day by cart and by foot. Long, lovely days across plains and mountain ranges, and at last across a desert place with great lion-colored dunes and a vast dome of blue pellucid sky. There the painted temple cliff city seeming a mirage but not a mirage. It was real. Through the centuries the cliff has fallen away in places by the process of erosion so that many of the antechambers and sometimes the inner chambers can be seen shimmering with soft color some distance away. When the traveler comes closer he may see the temples one by one and understand something of their meaning. The almost countless walls are painted to honor the Lord Buddha and show forth his glory. He appears as the great central figure in one after an-

Painting from the South Wall of Cave 139A, Tun Huang. Fogg Museum of Art, Harvard University.

other of his various paradises, surrounded by bodhisattvas, various guardians, his favorite disciples, and a host of angel-like apsarases.

Such temples were for Buddhism very much what the Romanesque and Gothic churches were for Christianity—visual holy books. Just as at Chartres one sees Christ with the four beasts of the Apocalypse, his twelve apostles, and scenes from his life, so at Tun Huang we see Buddha with his hierarchy, scenes from his life and the legends that surround it.

The chief deity of all these temples is of course the Lord Buddha. He in his various manifestations is the central figure on most of the altars whether they are at the back of the main temple hall or set into the niches of the earlier core pillars. He often appears as the middle figure of a trinity, often with two of the great bodhisattvas who come second in rank in the Buddhist hierarchy. Sometimes he has two or four of his favorite disciples in monks' robes and in addition to them two or four of the Guardian Kings in armor. Other attendant bodhisattvas stand or kneel like the lovely creature in the Fogg Museum of Harvard University. Apsarases, the heavenly dancing girls (pardonably mistaken for angels by Westerners), fly overhead in a plethora of fluttering draperies. These sculptured groups are painted in the same delicate colors as the walls and ceilings—colors which in the West we find in true fresco. The very early temples, the Wei temples, have a good deal of the soft orange and pink found in begonias; the T'ang temples are mostly a pale clear green, a pale clear blue and white; the Sung temples have a general soft pink and green tonality. In all three dynasties other colors are used for detail, but sparingly.

The walls are decorated in a series of panels sometimes vertical, sometimes horizontal. They are a kind of pictorial Buddhist Bible. Most common is the Buddha enthroned and holding court in his various paradises with his heavenly hosts about him. Smaller panels contain the countless scenes of his life and the legendary scenes of his former existences. You may see him throwing himself as a meal to a hungry tiger or balancing an elephant aloft on his right hand. These stories are endless.

The donors and donatrices of the temples appear in the costumes of their day. The early ones are tiny, and they increase in size until in the Sung Dynasty we find the life-size "King of Khotan" and his lady heading long processions of the royal offspring. The ceilings seem to billow like a tent. In the four corners are the Guardian Kings of the points of the compass. At the apex is a flat lotus flower, and the four triangular panels aspire to it sometimes in severe diapered patterns, sometimes with balanced figures. There is no end to the variety, but there is a holy radiance in all of them, something of the same radiance you will find in the cathedral of St. Mark's in Venice.

We in the West can see only isolated fragments of such things. It is like hearing a symphony in snatches, a note here, a half-phrase there. We are dimly aware there is more, and want it, but it goes by in the wind.

We describe Tun Huang as an introduction to Chinese religious painting. It is convenient and has a long history so that if a group of archaeologists could work there year in and year out they might ultimately give us a pretty clear history of Buddhist painting in China from the fifth century to the twentieth. Buddhist art in China, both sculpture and painting, was mostly anonymous, just as was medieval and Byzantine painting and sculpture in the West. Both East and West, art was the work of craftsmen, and the egoism of the present day engendered by the Renaissance has difficulty in even recognizing master craftsmen, as well as in realizing that in the service of God great painters both East and West were humble and that often a lesser painter without knowing it was inspired by a divine ecstasy. In this day, almost without knowing what we do, we seek out from small and almost un-

Monk Holding a Lotus Flower, fresco of the T'ang Dynasty (618–906).
Provenance: Turfan (Kyzyl). Metropolitan Museum of Art.

known places scraps and fragments of painting that were inspired. Your school books and too many lectures on Chinese painting will tell you that at best this religious painting was "provincial," a word which in classroom lingo means rather crude and inferior. This is not so. The cave temples of Tun Huang are, as were the cave temples of the Turfan oasis, one magnificent symphony after another.

The paintings of Tun Huang are not "provincial." The proof of this appeared recently. Liang Ssu-ch'eng found a wall painting at the Wu T'ai Shan a thousand miles and more away from Tun Huang which is exactly the same as the T'ang paintings at Tun Huang and only a few days' travel from the capital city of T'ang China. Anonymous church art—yes; provincial—no.

But there is an amusing divergence of human thought here. In the West, as far as painting and sculpture are concerned, we find the medievalist church painters anonymous and the Renaissance painters very, very egoistical. But in China the two things ran side by side—temple painters were usually anonymous, but secular and court painters were anything but anonymous for a good two thousand years. How do you account for that? The answer is simple, of course, but can be easily distorted. The temple painters were craftsmen, often inspired; the secular painters were self-consciously painters and desirous of making a name for themselves.

If we choose Tun Huang as an aspect of Chinese religious painting we must point out that this is merely a star exhibit. Look at the map of China. Think of our public libraries and remember that over that whole vast area there were big and little temples century in and century out. Some of the cave temples have survived. There were others. Many. The Confucians built magnificent temples, but without wall paintings. The Taoist in the matter of decoration seems to have imitated and elaborated the Buddhist painting, but mostly it has the emptiness of imitation and propaganda—when we speak of what we call art it is negligible. The Lamaist Buddhist painting is prodigious, less on walls than on hanging paintings called by us banners. Lamaist art is mostly a business of traditional craftsmen, always handsome decoration, with reflections of greatness, a manifestation not to be despised but on the contrary to be studied and admired as a vehicle which has preserved the elements of greatness.

These things must be noted, but there is no doubt that in the history of Chinese art as we see it in the mid-twentieth century the manifestation of religious painting in China is Buddhist. It was they who believed and burned like a flame, a flame so intense and passionate that it has burned some fifteen hundred years.

15. The Lovely Beasts

"About them frisking played
All beasts of the earth, since wild, and of all chase
In wood or wilderness, forest or den.
Sporting the lion ramped, and in his paw
Dandled the kid; bears, tigers, ounces, pards,
Gambolled before them; the unwieldy elephant,
To make them mirth, used all his might, and wreathed
His lithe proboscis . . ."

So DOES the poet Milton describe the animals as they behaved in the Garden of Eden, and in Western paintings of that garden certainly animals seem to be very much at peace with one another. Animals assemble in Oriental paintings of another garden to mourn at the death of Buddha, which was no death but merely the sleep in which he left the earthly scene. The animals appear at peace in these pictures too, but it is not quite the same thing because these Buddhist animals had only temporarily left off their natural feeding habits. Drawn together in common sorrow to have the Enlightened One go, they came to mourn and departed to devour.

What happened to the animals of the Garden of Eden when the Archangel Michael drove Adam and Eve out of it? The serpent was rebuked for his part in the affair and told he would forever crawl upon his belly and eat dust, but as far as we know he was not ordered out of it. Were the rest of the animals somehow affected by Adam and Eve's transgression? "And to every beast of the earth, and to every fowl of the air, and to everything that creepeth upon the earth, wherein there is life, I have given every green herb for meat: and it was so." A commentator on this passage says, "It doth not appear that either men or animals would have eaten flesh during the state of innocency." Whatever happened it is certain that Western carnivores took to eating flesh at a very early date and were for a time encouraged to feast on Christians publicly.

The animals of Buddhism present no such knotty problems. Buddha himself looked with sympathetic interest upon the animal world. He knew that the tiger in his stage of development must eat raw meat and drink blood. So compassionate was Buddha that on one occasion meeting a hungry tiger he cast himself down and became the tiger's supper. This incident occasionally appears in the small scenes in Lamaist paintings. That, of course, was thousands and thousands of years ago, but within our twentieth century a Japanese official posted in China sought to emulate Buddha and was found naked upon a mountainside outside Nanking. He had taken his clothes off, he explained, lest his cuff links give the tiger indigestion.

These tigers were encouraged to eat human flesh, but another Chinese tiger, the tiger of Chao-ch'eng-hsien, was brought to book for it. "Shan-hsi Chao-ch'eng-hsien yiu i ko lao p'o-tse." (In Shansi province, in the town of Chao-ch'eng, lived an old widow.) This is the first sentence of a tale which confronted students at the North China Language School in Peking in 1925. The old widow had a son who supported her by gathering faggots for firewood on the local mountain, or did so support her until he was eaten by a tiger.

When this kind of thing happens in the American scene, as it occasionally does in animal acts, or when a tormented elephant in a zoo turns upon its tormentor, the offending animal is instantly destroyed. It was different in Shansi. The old widow was more practical—she went off to the local magistrate and howled her plaint. The magistrate sent for the tiger and berated him soundly. The chief objection seemed to be that he had eaten the only son of the widow, thus removing her means of support. (Had he eaten only one of a large family there would probably have been no fuss about it at all.) As it was, the magistrate scolded him and bade him take care of the old widow. As the magistrate's sentence rolled out, the tiger bowed his head and bowed his head again, and for the rest of her life he deposited a fat deer upon the widow's doorstep every morning. Deer meat brings rather a higher price than faggots; so it all turned out for the best.

If you do not believe this story you may go to Chao-ch'eng-hsien, where you will find a painting of a tiger on the wall of the chief inn of that town and perhaps be convinced.

Living in Peking, your reason might inform you that the frightening creatures that screamed and scrambled over your roofs in the middle of the night were merely the neighbor's cats bent on making horrid love or indulging in a light supper of your favorite thrush—reason might inform you so, but it was still a comfort to have the Number One boy hastily build a small temple to propitiate the Fox Fairy of Nanyuan.

Foreigners in China soon learn that even serpents must not be killed within the precincts of a Buddhist temple, but it is puzzling to the foreigner to see serpents carefully caged and tended in the monastery of Tan Chih-ssu, and more puzzling

Tigers, attributed to Shih-t'ao (*ca.* 1650). On loan to the Metropolitan Museum of Art.

124

to see them occasionally placed in palanquins and carried off to Peking to visit an ailing parishioner.

These stories are examples of the way the twentieth century Chinese in general regard the animal world, and something of the same attitude you must adopt if you wish to enter the world of Chinese animals. It is true, of course, that a goodly number of Chinese enlightened by Western education at Oxford or Harvard, the kind of Chinese you are likely to meet, will assure you that China has outgrown such beliefs. But large as the number of Western-educated Chinese is, it is but a fraction of one per cent of the Chinese population, and if you will take your best-educated and most intelligent Chinese friend to the Maine woods you will discover an odd look in his eye if a fox or even a woodchuck puts in a sudden appearance.

The tiger seems to be the favorite carnivore of the Chinese. They admired the tiger much as the West admired the lion. (The Chinese did not know much about lions in the early days and accepted the winged version of the Near East to guard their tombs in the Han dynasty and a little later the Buddhist lion of India to guard the entrance gates of temples and the doorways of the mansions of the great.)

Aside from his private escapades the tiger became a symbol of physical strength and often appears as one of a pair of paintings or screens to balance a dragon, who when he appears with the tiger is a symbol of intellectual or spiritual strength.

A great many of the Chinese birds and animals are symbols of something, sometimes for no better reason than that their names make easy puns, and the Chinese have a deplorable passion for puns. The deer, for instance, is a symbol of wealth and often appears in paintings of birthday parties holding a lucky fungus in its mouth. Why? Because the Chinese ideograph, or character, for deer is pronounced "lu" and the character for riches is also pronounced "lu." The bat, generally considered in the West as an odious, smelly, blood-sucking little beast, is in China a symbol of happiness. Why? The character for bat is pronounced "fu" and the character for happiness is also pronounced "fu." It is a curious thing that if one has much to do with Chinese art, so accustomed does one become to the pretty bats which appear in countless textiles and porcelains that one forgets the Western idea of a bat and sees the real ones with Chinese eyes, noticing the delicate scallops of their wings, their gay and flickering flight, and their impish little faces. Very few species suck blood really—most of them are whickering around in pursuit of fat-bellied night moths and smaller insects.

The chief roles of the elephant and lion are associated with Buddhism, the elephant as the mount of the Bodhisattva Samantabhadra, known in China as P'u Hsien, the lion as the steed of the Bodhisattva Manjusri, known in China as Wen Shu. When these two deities appear as companions of Kuan Yin, that deity ap-

Landscape with Deer, album leaf in the style of the Sung Dynasty (960–1280). Metropolitan Museum of Art.

pears seated upon a large feline known as a *hou*, sometimes loosely described by Westerners as a blue lion.

The crane is always a symbol of long life, the feng huang (too often referred to as the Chinese phoenix) usually appears to emperors as an auspicious omen and prefers to light in the branches of the pawlonia tree.

The dignified tortoise is a symbol of longevity and appears upholding memorial steles, but the unlucky turtle is the symbol of a cuckold and appears in chalk drawings made by small and disrespectful boys upon the walls of houses. One must be wary of mentioning turtles. It is even improper to ask for a weather prophecy of a

Chinese. Why? Because the turtle knows what the weather will be. Why does the turtle know the weather? Because he is a cuckold. If this still seems complicated and obscure it must be explained, first, that in poetry a reference to clouds and rain, or snow and flowers, is a delicate euphemism for sexual intercourse, a matter the unhappy cuckold knows too much about; second, that this sad predicament is visited upon the turtle because in the Yuan dynasty the husbands of prostitutes served as runners for the establishment in which their wives prostituted and these runners were by sumptuary law required to wear green uniforms and hats vaguely suggesting the turtle. I do not know if this particular bit of lore can be found in any previous writing. It took a long time to extract it from contemporary Chinese scholars, who would perhaps prefer to remain anonymous and forego any credit due them.

In surveying birds and animals as symbols one should not overlook the fact that the Chinese selected birds and animals to represent the various ranks of officialdom from the emperor and empress on down to the ninth-degree officials. These symbols were prescribed by law, and we have tables of them with minor changes made from time to time throughout the Ming and Ch'ing dynasties. They were worn on official dress in the insignia which we call mandarin squares. This group of birds and animals, some real, some mythical, would make an extraordinary little zoological garden all by themselves. The emperor wears the dragon, the censors the ch'i-lin and the po-hsieh. Military officials wear animals, civil officials birds. It is impossible not to believe that the committees who selected them did not allow themselves a quiet grin when they selected the peacock for the third rank and the humble quail for the eighth rank. Other birds are the crane, the goose, pheasants gold and silver, the egret, the mandarin duck, the oriole, the long-tailed flycatcher. Among the lovely beasts are the lion, the tiger, the leopard, the bear, the rhinoceros, and the sea horse.

Let us consider a bit some of the species of this peculiar zoo and other species that might well be added to it. Some of these animals and birds, although great liberties have been taken in representing them, are real animals and birds that you can find in a natural-history book. Others are animals of the imagination, but so lifelike, so possible do some of these imaginary beasts and birds appear that quite sober and serious scholars quarrel humorlessly about them. Occasionally they make convincing identifications of them, as in the case of the feng huang, that gorgeous bird with plumes of five colors whose origin the Marquis Hachisuka and Captain Delacour tell us is the beautifully marked but dun-colored pheasant known in our day as Rhinehardt's ocellated argus pheasant. In this case we can see how the Chinese imagination and the Chinese painters move from an actual living bird to the creation of a superbird which looks so probable that we might hope to find it living in some tropic Oriental jungle. The feng huang appears in the earliest Chinese literature—the Four Books and the Five Classics, and it doubtless has a much earlier history—surely its ancestors appear among the conventionalized birds of the Shang bronzes.

The early Chinese references make agreeable reading. In the *Shih Ching*, or "Book of Poetry," we find:

> "The male and female phoenix fly about,
>   Their wings rustling,
>   While they settle in their proper resting place.
>   Many are your admirable officers, O king,
>   Ready to be employed by you,
>   Loving you, the Son of Heaven."

> "The male and female phoenix fly about,
>   Their wings rustling,
>   As they soar up to heaven.
>   Many are your admirable officers, O king,
>   Waiting for your commands,
>   And loving the multitudes of the people."

> "The male and female phoenix give out
>   their notes,
>   On that lofty bridge.
>   The dryandras grow,
>   On these eastern slopes,
>   They grow luxuriantly;
>   And harmoniously the notes resound."

In the *Shu Ching*, or "Book of Historical Documents": "When the nine parts of the service according to the emperor's arrangements have all been performed, the male and female phoenix come with their measured gambolings into the court."

There is a remark about the feng huang in the Confucian *Analects*—a rather dreary one: "The Master said, 'the Feng bird does not come; the river sends no map:—it is all over with me.' "

The chief disciple of Lao Tzu gives us a piece of pseudo-natural history that in one point touches the truth: "In the south there is a bird. It is a kind of phoenix. Do you know it? It started from the south sea to fly to the north sea. Except on the wu-t'ung tree, it would not alight. It would eat nothing but the fruit of the bamboo, drink nothing but the purest spring water."

128

Dragons and Landscape (detail), in the style of Ch'en Jung (*fl. ca.* 1235). Metropolitan Museum of Art.

Then there is the evidence of that most lovely philosopher's geography and natural history combined, the *Shan Hai Ching*, or "Mountain and Sea Classic." Here we are told of the feng huang indeed: "Again five hundred *li* to the east there is a mountain called Red Cave [*Tan-hsueh*]. At the top there is a great deal of gold and jade."

"The Red River (*Tan-shui*) comes out here and flows south and goes into the P'o Sea (*P'o-hai*).

"There is a bird whose shape is like a cock. It has five colors and stripes. It is called feng-huang. (As the dragon is the chief of the animals, the phoenix is the chief of the birds. It is the symbol of happiness.) The stripes on the head are called virtue; the stripes on the wings, justice; on the back, politeness; those on the breast are called humanity; those on the stomach, honesty. This bird drinks and eats, sings and dances, by itself. When it appears the world enjoys peace."

These are the earliest references to the feng huang. As time went on many new attributes and stories surrounded it. Whenever one appeared, the event would be reported to the emperor at once, and there would be a great celebration, on a national scale. The name of a place or the designation of the emperor's reign might be changed for such an event. We can find many such records in the dynasty histories. The *Tz'u Yuan* ("Chinese Encyclopedic Dictionary") gives the five colors of the feng huang: blue, yellow, red, white, and black.

This is part of the Chinese pedigree for the feng huang. The surprising thing is that so many characteristics of the seemingly fanciful bird of Chinese legend check with characteristics of Rhinehardt's ocellated argus. Delacour, stern ornithologist, sees the likeness in the very fancy description the Chinese give. In cold blood he points out: "From literature, the Phoenix's characteristics can be summarized as follows: 'It is a ground bird; it takes several years to reach maturity; sexes are different; it has the head of a cock, the neck of a snake, the chin of a swallow, the back of a tortoise and the tail of a fish; it has five colors and reaches a length of six feet.' " Westerners are not taught to describe birds in such a way, but Captain Delacour has the adaptability to see that in its way this is a very good description of the bird. Certainly it has a head as proud as the proudest cock; certainly it has the neck of a snake; certainly it has the chin of a swallow and there the Chinese have been better observers than we—(look next time at that full chin all swallows have); the back of a tortoise (here the reference is to the diapered markings); and the tail of a fish. The poetic links are all there; and while Dr. Chapman might have taken the Chinese to task for not using a proper terminology I am sure he would have smiled with pleasure at the Chinese description.

Like the feng huang the dragon appears in the earliest Chinese literature and like the feng huang must be among the strange beasts on the Shang bronzes. The Shang collections of birds and animals is a wonderful thing in itself, but it is better to keep out of that prehistoric jungle when we deal with the birds and animals of Chinese painting. Likewise, the Chinese dragon so brilliantly articulated is a believable animal. The Chinese story of the great carp swimming upstream until he vaults Heaven's gate and becomes a dragon gives us a hint of the origin of this creature, especially as we have pictures of the carp taking the leap with his scales shining and filaments streaming feverishly from his jaws. Imagine this carp like an insect emerging from its chrysalid or like a tadpole changing—suddenly putting out its legs, suddenly extending its length, suddenly growing legs, suddenly possessed of such lightness that it can transfer its life from the heavy water of sea and stream and move quite naturally into the lighter clouds and mists, and there you have a plausible genesis of the dragon as we see him in Chinese painting.

Like the feng huang, the dragon appears in the classics, but his subsequent history is far more complicated, and he appears in many guises and with many interpretations. He was in China long before Buddhism came, but he has become invested with the aura that surrounds the Nagas of Buddhism. The Taoist religion has scores of Dragon kings—and in legend his amours, never talked about, must almost have rivaled those of Zeus, since there are no less than nine combining forms well described by Mrs. Ayscough in *The Chinese Mirror.*

The West considers him chiefly in his two most conspicuous roles: (1) the symbol of air and mist and water and of spiritual strength; (2) the symbol of the Emperor of China.

The ch'i lin is more in evidence in recent centuries than in ancient times. He is usually translated as unicorn. Foreigners seeking to explain the marvels they found in China and snatching at the best analogies they could, compared the feng

Feng huang, Ming Dynasty (1368–1644) or earlier. Metropolitan Museum of Art.

huang to the phoenix and the ch'i lin to the unicorn. The feng huang and the phoenix are two different and very brilliant birds, and no amount of research has yet found or is likely to find a common ancestor for them. The ch'i lin and the unicorn are even further apart both in character and appearance. The only likeness is that they both have a horn but a horn as different as noses. They have nothing to do with each other at all.

We will not speak of unicorns but of the ch'i lin, which is a lovely beast. A really lovely beast. There are those that would like to connect him with the legendary animal who came out of the Yellow River with the eight diagrams upon his skin. If he appears in the wonderful zoo of the Shang bronzes nobody has as yet detected him. His pedigree is difficult. Pedigrees surely are a human convention, a device to make the individual important. For the same reason, perhaps, have they made pedigrees for domestic animals? Human beings arbitrarily decide what the qualifications are for a prize hog. There is very little logic in it—they set down rules on a physical basis for hogs, and we all conform to them. Pedigrees for human beings, of course, can't as yet be done quite that way. What is a pedigree for a human being? Record of family continuity? Public eminence? All very admirable, but if you come right down to it, can you have a human being without ancestors? Can you have a ch'i lin without forebears?

Eschew the ch'i lin's pedigree and meet him as he has been most conspicuous in the recent Ming and Ch'ing dynasties, a matter of a mere five hundred and fifty years. The ch'i lin, we are told, is a linked name as is the feng huang. The male is the *ch'i*—the female the *lin*. In general form it resembles a stag (it does not remotely, but scholars tell us so).

The naturalist surveying it notes that it has the hooves of a horse and the tail of an ox. It has five colors in its skin, red, yellow, blue, white, and black. It is twelve cubits high. Its voice is like the sound of bells. Its character, for all it looks so fearsome, is sweet. It does not tread on insects. It appears only to emperors of good character to inspirit them or when a sage is to be born. "The unicorn envelops itself with benevolence, and crowns itself with rectitude."

This is the talk about it and it may very well be true. In any case it gallops lightly across the Chinese pictorial scene for many hundred years, and more than one has galloped into the Metropolitan collections. He is a beast of good omen, and if you do not already know him well, acquaint yourself and make friends with him.

Sometimes it seems puzzling that human beings with all the marvelous real beasts and birds and insects living right beside them create for themselves the beasts of the imagination. And then you must look out. Because once created these fantasy beasts are more real than the cow at your back door. The ones we are

132

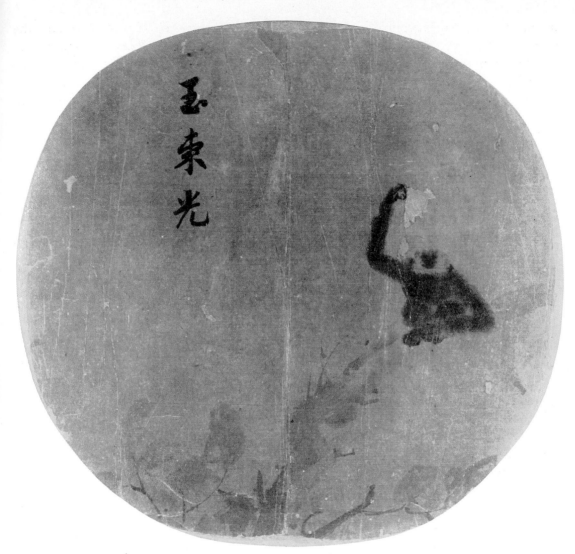

The Moaning of the Monkey, album leaf attributed to Wen Hsin, Yuan Dynasty (1280–1368). Metropolitan Museum of Art.

familiar with in the West, the winged horse, Pegasus, the dragon that glowered over Andromeda, and the dragon that confronted St. George are quite real. The phoenix advertises an insurance company, the unicorn as he appears in England, "the Lion and the Unicorn," is very common. We are superior and wise and have put the beasts in their place, to be sure—but there are the beasts as real as any creature you will see at the zoo—and perhaps more real.

But you must learn about the Chinese beasts and indeed about the Chinese demons. Compare a medieval dragon with a Chinese dragon. Both are fantastic, but ever and always your Chinese dragon and all the other beasts are logical creatures. The Western dragon is a lumpy, unwieldy creature, somewhat pinned together. The Chinese dragon out of glorious fish into a creature of air is far more logical, far more believable.

A man can be sensible and make his own private world secure with facts—and there are enough wonders of bird and beast and insect life to satisfy him. There are enough real animals at the zoo for any man to be sure of, but from the beginning of civilization man has invented fanciful beasts. Why not? They are lovely beasts, and the Chinese beasts are the most lovely and lovable of all.